STUDENT UNIT GUIDE

AS Chemistry
UNIT 2

Edexcel Nuffield

Unit 2: Bonding and Reactions

Frank Harriss and Philip Jackson

Philip Allan Updates
Market Place
Deddington
Oxfordshire
OX15 0SE

Orders
Bookpoint Ltd, 130 Milton Park, Abingdon, Oxfordshire, OX14 4SB
tel: 01235 827720
fax: 01235 400454
e-mail: uk.orders@bookpoint.co.uk
Lines are open 9.00 a.m.–5.00 p.m., Monday to Saturday, with a 24-hour message answering service. You can also order through the Philip Allan Updates website: www.philipallan.co.uk

© Philip Allan Updates 2004

ISBN-13: 978-0-86003-948-8
ISBN-10: 0-86003-948-X

All rights reserved; no part of this publication may be reproduced, stored in a retrieval system, or transmitted, in any form or by any means, electronic, mechanical, photocopying, recording or otherwise without either the prior written permission of Philip Allan Updates or a licence permitting restricted copying in the United Kingdom issued by the Copyright Licensing Agency Ltd, 90 Tottenham Court Road, London W1T 4LP.

This guide has been written specifically to support students preparing for the Edexcel Nuffield AS Chemistry Unit 2 examination. The content has been neither approved nor endorsed by Edexcel and remains the sole responsibility of the authors.

Printed by MPG Books, Bodmin

Philip Allan Updates' policy is to use papers that are natural, renewable and recyclable products and made from wood grown in sustainable forests. The logging and manufacturing processes are expected to conform to the environmental regulations of the country of origin.

Edexcel (Nuffield) Unit 2

Contents

Introduction
About this guide 4
How to use this guide 4
Revision and examination technique 5

Content Guidance
About this section 12
Redox reactions and oxidation numbers 13
The halogens 16
Covalency 22
Bond breaking 26
Hydrocarbons 31
Halogenoalkanes 37
Intermolecular forces 40

Questions and Answers
About this section 46

Section A
Q1 Bromine 47
Q2 Hydrogen iodide 49
Q3 Phosgene 53
Q4 Cracking 57
Q5 Halogenoalkanes 61
Q6 Nitrogen and ammonia 65

Section B
Q7 Comprehension 68

Introduction

About this guide

This guide is designed to help you prepare for the second Nuffield AS Chemistry unit test, which examines the content of **Unit 2: Bonding and Reactions**.

The aim of this guide is to provide you with a clear understanding of the requirements of the unit and to advise you on how best to meet those requirements.

The book is divided into the following sections:
- This **Introduction**, which outlines revision and examination technique, showing you how to prepare for the unit test.
- **Content Guidance**, which provides a summary of all the 'chemical ideas' covered in Unit 2.
- **Questions and Answers**, in which you will find questions in the same style as in the unit test, followed by the answers of two students, one of whom is likely to get an A grade, the other a C/D grade. Examiner's comments follow each of these answers.

How to use this guide

- Begin by reading the section 'Revision and examination technique' in this Introduction.
- Decide on the amount of time you have available for chemistry revision.
- Allocate suitable amounts of time to:
  — each section of the Content Guidance, giving the most time to the areas that seem most unfamiliar
  — the questions in the Questions and Answers section
- Draw up a revision timetable, allocating the time for questions later in your timetable.
- When revising sections of the Content Guidance:
  — read the guidance and look at corresponding sections in your notes and textbooks
  — write your own revision notes
  — try questions from past unit tests and from other sources, such as the *Students' Book*
- When using the Questions and Answers:
  — try to answer the question yourself
  — then look at the students' answers, together with your own, and try to work out the best answer
  — then look at the examiner's comments

Edexcel (Nuffield) Unit 2

Revision and examination technique

How do I find what to learn?
Well, we hope this book will be useful to you! Other sources are:
- the specification. This is the definitive one. If it's not in the skills section of the specification, it won't be in the paper! However, the specification is written in 'examiner-speak', so it might not always be absolutely clear what is required. This guide should help you to interpret the unit content — every specification point is covered in the Content Guidance section.
- the summaries of Key Principles at the end of the topics in the *Students' Book*.
- your own and your teacher's notes. Preparation for an exam is not just something you do shortly before you take the paper. It should be an integral part of your daily work in chemistry.

How much of the *Students' Book* do I need to learn?
You will need most of this, except:
- the fine detail of experimental procedure
- background reading
- sections 6.6, 6.7 and 7.1, which are expressly excluded in the specification

General revision tips
Revision is a personal thing
What works for one person does not necessarily work for another. You should by now have some idea about which methods suit you, but here are a few ways to set out your revision notes:
- mind maps — ideas radiate out from a central point and are linked together; some people like to colour these in
- notes with bullet points and headings
- small cards with a limited 'bite-size' amount of material on each

Make a plan
Divide your material into sections (the Content Guidance section will be useful here). Then:
- work out how much time you have available before the exam
- allocate each section as much time as you can, bearing in mind which you feel you nearly understand and which are the most difficult
- fit this in with any revision your teacher is going to do — ask him or her for a summary

Write, write, write!
Whatever you do, make sure that your revision is *active*, not just flipping over the pages saying 'yeah, yeah, I know this already'. Write more revision notes, test yourself (or each other), *try questions*.

Test yourself
- The review questions in the *Students' Book* are useful 'drill exercises' on topics, but are not all like exam questions.
- Past papers are available and they give you a good indication of what you will be facing.
- The Questions and Answers section of this book is designed for this purpose.

Know the enemy — the exam paper

Hopefully, since you will have prepared properly, you will be able to look on the exam as an opportunity to show what you can do, rather than as a battle! Be aware, however, that you must prepare yourself for an exam just as you would for an important sporting contest — be focused. Work hard right through the 90 minutes and don't dwell on difficulties — put them behind you. Try to emerge feeling worn out but happy that you have done your best, even if you have found it difficult (others will probably feel the same way). Then forget it and don't have a postmortem.

Sections A and B

Section A usually consists of four structured questions. Each question has a 'theme' and includes both short-answer and longer-answer parts. Section A is worth 45 marks.

Section B is a comprehension exercise, worth 15 marks. There is a passage to read and some short questions based on the content of the passage. Finally, you have to write a summary (within a certain word limit) of some aspect of the passage. Here you will be assessed on the quality of your written English.

Nuffield is all about learning chemistry through experiment, so it is right that the exam questions should reflect this. However, some will be based on chemistry in everyday life and others will be more theoretical.

Sometimes the context will come from the *Students' Book*; sometimes it will be a new one. Look carefully at the 'stem' (the introduction at the top of the question). Most of the important facts here will be needed somewhere in the question. Sometimes, small, additional stems are added later. These are important too.

60 marks in 90 minutes

Most people *just* finish this unit test within the time. On the paper you are advised to spend 55 minutes on section A and 35 minutes on section B. However, section B can be time consuming and most students find that they need to spend more than 35 minutes; therefore they spend less time on section A. Work out the timing strategy that best suits you by practising past papers.

Dealing with different types of question

Short-answer questions

These are the most straightforward, but remember:
- look at the marks available — make one good point per mark.

- look at the number of lines — this gives *some* idea of the length of answer required. Of course, handwriting varies greatly in size, but if you have written two words and there are three lines, you can assume you have not written enough to score full marks!
- don't 'hedge your bets' — if you give two alternative answers, you will not get the marks unless *both* are right. For example, if the answer is 'hydrogen bond' and you write 'hydrogen bond or permanent dipole attractions', you will score zero.
- read the question — don't answer a question that you have made up! Examiners do have kind hearts really, and they are genuinely sorry when they have to award zero for an answer containing good chemistry that is not relevant to the question asked. This is a problem with units that are examined twice a year. There are lots of past papers around, all asking slightly different questions on the same subject-matter. It's all too easy to give the answer to last year's question.

Longer-answer questions
The same rules apply about marks, lines and reading the question. In addition:
- think before you write — perhaps jot down a few points in the margin. Try to make your points logically.
- punch those points — if you have read any mark-schemes you will see that they give examiners advice on the weakest answer that will still just score the mark. Make sure your points are made well and win the mark without requiring a second's hesitation by the examiner.
- try to write clear sentences (though bullet points might be appropriate on some occasions).
- be sure you do not re-state the question — don't use words or phrases directly from the question as part of your explanation.

Comprehension question
- Read the passage straight through to get the general sense.
- Reread the question and fix in your mind which section of the passage you are being asked to précis.
- Read the passage again more carefully, looking for key points for your summary — usually there will be seven or eight. Some students like to highlight these key points; others like to note them down.
- The next stage is to write a rough draft linking your key points with proper English. Count the words. If you have used too many, you will have to edit your summary to shorten it. There are penalties for using too many words — usually 1 mark is deducted for every five words above the set total, which is usually 100 or 120 words. If you are far short of the total, it is likely that you have missed out some key points.
- Now write out the finished version on *alternate lines*. This makes it easier for the examiner to mark and easier for you to make alterations. Write the number of words used at the end. Do not be tempted to tell a fib, for instance by saying you have used 120 words when you have used 135. The examiner *will* check.

- There are usually 6 marks for the key points and 2 marks for good English (and it has to be *really* good). Remember to cross out your rough draft so that the examiner does not mark it by mistake.

Command words in questions
A lot of care is taken in choosing which of these words to use, so note them carefully:
- 'state', 'write down', 'give' and 'name' require short answers only
- 'describe' requires an accurate account of the main points, but no explanation
- 'explain' or 'justify' requires chemical reasons for the statement given
- 'suggest' means that you are not expected to know the answer but you should be able to work it out from what you do know
- 'giving reason(s)' requires you to explain why you chose to answer as you did (if 'reasons' in the plural is stated, judge the number required from the number of marks)

Avoid vague answers
Sometimes it is clear that the candidate knows quite a lot about the topic but his or her answer is not focused. Avoid these words:
- 'it' (e.g. 'it is bigger') — give the name of the thing you are describing, otherwise it may not be clear which object in the question is being referred to
- 'harmful' — if you mean 'toxic' or 'poisonous', say so!
- 'environmentally friendly' — say *why* it benefits the environment
- 'expensive' — always justify this word with a reason

Be careful with chemical particles — always think twice whenever you write 'particle', 'atom', 'molecule' or 'ion', and check that you are using the correct term.

If in doubt, write something
Try to avoid leaving any gaps. Have a go at every answer. If you are not sure, write something that seems to be sensible chemistry. As you will see from the Questions and Answers section, some questions have a variety of possible answers — the only answer that definitely scores zero is a blank.

Diagrams
You would be amazed at some of the diagrams examiners have to mark, so please:
- read the question. The answer is not always a reflux condenser! If it is an apparatus you know, then it is relatively straightforward. If you have to design something, look for clues in the question.
- make it clear and neat. Use a pencil and a ruler, and have a soft rubber handy to erase any errors.
- make sure it looks like real apparatus (which never has square corners, for example). Some apparatus drawn in exams would test the skill of the most proficient glass-blower.
- draw a cross-section, so that gases can have a clear path through. Don't carelessly leave any gaps where gases could leak out.

- think of safety. Don't suggest heating an enclosed apparatus, which would explode. If a poisonous gas is given off, show it being released in a fume cupboard.
- always label your diagram, especially if the question tells you to. Important things to label are substances and calibrated vessels (e.g. syringes or measuring cylinders).

Calculations

It is easy to make mistakes, especially under the pressure of exams. So, set out the steps in your calculations clearly. Then you will get most of the marks if you make a slight mistake and the examiner can see what you are doing. Examiners operate a system called 'transferred error' whereby, once an error has been made, the rest of the calculation scores marks if the method is correct from then on.

When you write down your numerical answer, check:
- **units** — most physical quantities have them, for example $g\,mol^{-1}$, $kJ\,mol^{-1}$
- **sign** (remember that oxidation states and ΔH values must be shown as '+' if they are positive)
- **significant figures** — you may be expected to analyse uncertainties more carefully in your practical work, but in exam papers all you have to do is to give the same number of significant figures as the data in the question

Content Guidance

The material in this section summarises the chemical concepts from **Unit 2: Bonding and Reactions**. Note that each section of the Nuffield specification brings in chemical ideas from a variety of topic areas. This content guidance section is divided into chemical topics, which in some cases link ideas from more than one section of the specification.

Summary of content

Redox reactions: redox reactions and oxidation numbers

Halogens: physical properties of the halogens; chemical properties of the halogens; chemical properties of the halides; chemical properties of the hydrogen halides

Covalency: covalent bonding and dot-and-cross diagrams; shapes of molecules; dative covalency; electronegativity

Bond breaking: bond energies; reversible reactions; Le Chatelier's principle

Hydrocarbons: naming alkanes; reactions of alkanes, including free-radical substitution; naming alkenes; reactions of alkenes, including electrophilic addition

Halogenoalkanes: naming halogenoalkanes; reactions of halogenoalkanes, including nucleophilic substitution

Intermolecular forces: van der Waals forces, permanent dipole attractions, hydrogen bonding

How much of this do I need to learn?

The answer is, virtually all of it. It has been pared down to the absolute essentials. If you need any more detail on any aspect, you should look in your textbooks or notes.

Edexcel (*Nuffield*) Unit 2

Redox reactions and oxidation numbers

Definitions and examples of redox reactions

Redox is a shortening of two words, **reduction** and **oxidation**. It is the name given to one of the most important types of chemical reaction. At GCSE you will have learnt some simple examples of, and definitions for, redox reactions. For example, oxidation is the gain of oxygen and reduction is the loss of oxygen. This can be shown by the reaction between magnesium and copper oxide:

$$Mg(s) + CuO(s) \longrightarrow MgO(s) + Cu(s)$$

- Magnesium has gained oxygen and is thus oxidised.
- Copper oxide has lost oxygen and is thus reduced.
- Magnesium is the reducing agent. (All metals are reducing agents.)
- Copper oxide is the oxidising agent.

Another simple example is when magnesium is burnt in air:

$$2Mg(s) + O_2(g) \longrightarrow 2MgO(s)$$

Magnesium is oxidised; therefore oxygen must be reduced. The product, magnesium oxide, is ionic. It contains Mg^{2+} ions and O^{2-} ions. Therefore, during oxidation, a magnesium atom becomes a magnesium ion by losing two electrons:

$$Mg \longrightarrow Mg^{2+} + 2e^-$$

During reduction, an oxygen atom becomes an oxide ion by gaining two electrons:

$$O + 2e^- \longrightarrow O^{2-}$$

Tip Remember '**oilrig**': **o**xidation **i**s **l**oss (of electrons); **r**eduction **i**s **g**ain (of electrons).

Oxidation numbers

Every element in every substance can be assigned an **oxidation number**. This useful concept allows us to describe how oxidised an element is. An element that has an oxidation number of +5 (e.g. the nitrogen in HNO_3) is more oxidised than when it has an oxidation number of −3 (e.g. the nitrogen in NH_3). We say that the nitrogen in the nitric acid is in a higher **oxidation state**. The more positive the oxidation number, the higher is the oxidation state. Oxidation numbers are useful in balancing redox equations.

Common errors include not giving a sign, or placing it after the number.
- You *must always* give the sign (e.g. +5, −3). *All* oxidation numbers (apart from zero) have a sign, even positive ones.
- The sign *must* go *before* the number. Putting it after the number (e.g. 3+, 2−) means that you are assigning an ionic charge, not an oxidation number.

There are some basic rules that you need to know for working out oxidation numbers:
- An uncombined element (e.g. chlorine, Cl_2, and magnesium, Mg) always has an oxidation number of 0.
- Hydrogen in compounds is always +1, except in metal hydrides (e.g. sodium hydride, NaH), when it is –1.
- Oxygen in compounds is always –2, except in peroxides (e.g. sodium peroxide, Na_2O_2), when it is –1.
- In *simple* ionic compounds such as sodium chloride, NaCl, the oxidation numbers of the elements are the same as their ionic charges. Therefore, in NaCl the oxidation number of Na⁺ is +1 and that of Cl⁻ is –1. A group 2 element such as magnesium has an oxidation number of +2 in its compounds, while a group 3 element such as aluminium has an oxidation number of +3 in its compounds.
- The oxidation numbers in a compound always add up to zero. For example, in aluminium chloride, $AlCl_3$, the aluminium is +3 and the three chlorides are *each* –1. Adding gives: +3 + 3(–1) = 0. If the sum does not add up to zero, then you have done something wrong.
- The sum of the oxidation numbers in more complicated ions adds up to the charge on the ion. In ions such as sulphate, SO_4^{2-}, sulphite, SO_3^{2-} and nitrate, NO_3^-, while the oxygen has an oxidation number of –2 (see the rule above), you have to do a small sum to work out the oxidation number of the sulphur or the nitrogen. For example, let the oxidation number of the sulphur in SO_4^{2-} be x. Therefore:

$x + 4(-2) = -2$

$x = +6$

So the oxidation number of the sulphur in SO_4^{2-} is +6.

Tip Don't just guess at oxidation numbers in ions such as these. They need to be worked out and you need to practise doing this.

Stock notation and naming compounds

Oxidation numbers are often used in naming compounds. You might remember iron(II) oxide, FeO, and iron(III) oxide, Fe_2O_3, from GCSE. The Roman numerals in brackets are the oxidation states of the iron in these compounds. In other words, they are equivalent to the oxidation numbers of the iron:
- In iron(II) oxide, the oxidation number of the iron is +2 (the iron ion is Fe^{2+}).
- In iron(III) oxide, the oxidation number of the iron is +3 (the iron ion is Fe^{3+}).

The Roman numerals are examples of **Stock notation**. The iron in iron(III) oxide has a higher oxidation number than the iron in iron(III) oxide. Therefore, it is in a higher oxidation state, that is, it is more oxidised.

Anions are named in a similar way:
- Sulphate, SO_4^{2-}, is more correctly called sulphate(VI).
- Sulphite, SO_3^{2-}, is more correctly called sulphate(IV).

Tip Don't be intimidated by these Roman numerals — they just indicate the oxidation number.

It is a good idea to think of as many compounds of an element (e.g. nitrogen, chlorine and sulphur) as you can and for each compound work out the name, formula, correct

Stock notation name and the oxidation number of the element. This is shown below for nitrogen.

Oxidation number	Formula	Original name	Modern name
+5	NO_3^-	Nitrate	Nitrate(V)
+4	NO_2	Nitrogen dioxide	Nitrogen(IV) oxide
+3	NO_2^-	Nitrite	Nitrate(III)
+2	NO	Nitrogen monoxide (nitric oxide)	Nitrogen(II) oxide
+1	N_2O	Dinitrogen monoxide (nitrous oxide)	Nitrogen(I) oxide
0	N_2	Nitrogen	Nitrogen
−1	NH_2OH	Hydroxylamine	Hydroxylamine
−2	N_2H_4	Hydrazine	Hydrazine
−3	NH_3	Ammonia	Ammonia
−3	NH_4^+	Ammonium ion	Ammonium ion

This shows just how many different oxidation numbers one element can have. Not all elements have this many — for example, group 1 and group 2 metals have only one oxidation number each.

Redox in terms of oxidation number

- Oxidation is an *increase* in oxidation number.
- Reduction is a *decrease* in oxidation number.

We can see this if we re-examine one of our earlier reactions in terms of oxidation number:

$$Mg(s) + CuO(s) \longrightarrow MgO(s) + Cu(s)$$

- The magnesium is oxidised. Its oxidation number changes from 0 in Mg to +2 in MgO — an increase.
- The copper is reduced. Its oxidation number changes from +2 in CuO to 0 in Cu — a decrease.

Balancing redox equations

There is a simple rule. The increase in oxidation number (in the oxidation part of the equation) must balance exactly the decrease in oxidation number (in the reduction part of the equation).

An example often used by examiners is the oxidation, in acid conditions, of iron(II) to iron(III) by the powerful oxidiser manganate(VII), MnO_4^-.

Tip There is an increase in oxidation number, so this must be the oxidation part of the reaction.

The unbalanced equation looks like this:

$Fe^{2+}(aq) + MnO_4^-(aq) + H^+(aq) \longrightarrow Fe^{3+}(aq) + Mn^{2+}(aq) + H_2O(l)$

The oxidation number of the iron changes from +2 to +3 — an increase of 1. The oxidation number of manganese in manganate(VII) is +7. (The Stock notation tells us this, but we could have worked it out anyway.) In Mn^{2+} the oxidation number of manganese is +2. Therefore, the oxidation number of the manganese decreases by 5.

However, the increase in oxidation number must balance the decrease. There is an increase of 1 for each iron(II) changing to iron(III). So, an overall increase of 5 will be given by five iron(II) ions changing to five iron(III) ions:

$5Fe^{2+}(aq) + MnO_4^-(aq) + H^+(aq) \longrightarrow 5Fe^{3+}(aq) + Mn^{2+}(aq) + H_2O(l)$

The increase in oxidation number now equals the decrease — the redox part of the equation is balanced, but there is another step in writing the overall balanced equation.

Notice that we have not mentioned the hydrogen or the oxygen. This is because their oxidation numbers do not change. However, the four oxygens from the MnO_4^- join with the H^+ to form four water molecules. The final equation looks like this:

$5Fe^{2+}(aq) + MnO_4^-(aq) + 8H^+(aq) \longrightarrow 5Fe^{3+}(aq) + Mn^{2+}(aq) + 4H_2O(l)$

Therefore, the stages in balancing a redox equation are as follows:
- Work out the changes in oxidation number.
- Make the total increase in oxidation number equal the total decrease (by multiplying, as with iron above).
- Balance the number of the other elements, for example hydrogen and oxygen.

Tip To check that you have got it right, add up the overall charge on the left-hand side and the overall charge on the right-hand side. They should be equal. In the example above they are both 17+.

The halogens

Physical properties of the halogens

The physical properties of the halogens are summarised in the following table.

Name	Formula	Melting point/°C	Boiling point/°C	Appearance/ state at room temperature	Electron arrangement
Fluorine	F_2	−220	−188	Pale yellow gas	$1s^2 2s^2 2p^5$
Chlorine	Cl_2	−101	−35	Green/yellow gas	$1s^2 2s^2 2p^6 3s^2 3p^5$
Bromine	Br_2	−7	59	Deep red/brown liquid	$1s^2 2s^2 2p^6 3s^2 3p^6 3d^{10} 4s^2 4p^5$
Iodine	I_2	114	184	Grey crystalline solid	$1s^2 2s^2 2p^6 3s^2 3p^6 3d^{10} 4s^2 4p^6 4d^{10} 5s^2 5p^5$

- The elements are diatomic — there are two atoms in each molecule.
- As the group is descended, the melting points and boiling points of the elements increase. This is because the number of electrons increases down the group, which increases the van der Waals forces *between* the molecules. Therefore, increasingly more energy is needed to pull the *molecules* away from each other — hence the increase in melting and boiling points.
- The increase in the number of electron shells as the group is descended means that the atoms increase in size down the group. Fluorine atoms are quite small; iodine atoms are much larger.

Atom	Atomic radius/nm	Ion	Ionic radius/nm
F	0.071	F⁻	0.133
Cl	0.099	Cl⁻	0.180
Br	0.114	Br⁻	0.195
I	0.133	I⁻	0.215

- For any given halogen atom, the corresponding halide anion is bigger because it has an extra electron (completing the *p* sub-shell). This means that there is greater repulsion between the outer electrons, which move further apart, increasing the radius.

Uses of halogens and their compounds

Of all the halogens, chlorine (and its compounds) has the most uses. Fluorine is also widely used, but bromine and iodine less so. It is probably a good idea to learn one example of a use for each halogen and a use for one compound of each halogen.

Halogen	Use	Halogen compound	Use
Fluorine	Manufacture of UF_6 to separate uranium isotopes	Fluorocarbons Sodium fluoride	Refrigerants, anaesthetics PTFE (Teflon) Added to toothpaste and water supplies to arrest the development of tooth decay in children
Chlorine	Industrial oxidant to manufacture bromine	HCl Sodium chlorate(I) Chloroethene Trichlorophenol	Removing rust from steel Bleach Monomer of PVC Antiseptic
Bromine	Making fire retardants	Bromomethane	Agricultural pest control
Iodine	Antiseptic for cuts and scratches	Potassium iodide	Animal feed additive

Chemical properties of the halogens

Halogens are powerful oxidising agents; they take electrons away from other elements. The ability to do this — their reactivity — decreases as the group is descended.

Fluorine is the most reactive non-metal and is not included in school chemistry courses. Iodine is the least reactive you will come across, as astatine is not covered by the specification.

Displacement reactions

The more reactive the halogen, the greater the ease with which it takes electrons from other elements (oxidises them), including other halogens.

Chlorine can take an electron from bromide and iodide ions. The chlorine atoms in the chlorine molecules become chloride ions; the bromide and iodide ions become bromine and iodine atoms, which join to form bromine and iodine molecules:

$$2Br^-(aq) + Cl_2(aq) \rightarrow 2Cl^-(aq) + Br_2(aq)$$
$$2I^-(aq) + Cl_2(aq) \rightarrow 2Cl^-(aq) + I_2(aq)$$

A simple explanation is that chlorine is more reactive than bromine and iodine and can displace them from their salts. More correctly, chlorine is the more powerful oxidiser and can oxidise the bromide and iodide ions — their oxidation numbers increase from –1 to 0.

Bromine is a more powerful oxidiser than iodine and oxidises iodide to iodine:

$$2I^-(aq) + Br_2(aq) \rightarrow 2Br^-(aq) + I_2(aq)$$

Bromine cannot oxidise chloride to chlorine.

When you do experiments on this topic it is often difficult to make out the colour change (a yellow/orange solution becomes a slightly deeper yellow/orange solution). This is made easier by adding a hydrocarbon solvent, such as cyclohexane, and mixing. The halogen dissolves preferentially in the hydrocarbon solvent and the colour becomes concentrated. This is particularly useful if iodine is produced, because in the hydrocarbon solvent iodine is a beautiful pink/purple colour.

Disproportionation

Disproportionation is a special example of a redox reaction, in which an element is both oxidised and reduced *at the same time*.

The reaction of chlorine with cold sodium hydroxide

$$Cl_2(aq) + 2OH^-(aq) \rightarrow Cl^-(aq) + ClO^-(aq) + H_2O(l)$$

- The oxidation numbers of oxygen and hydrogen stay the same, at –2 and +1 respectively, so they are not involved in the redox process.
- The oxidation number of chlorine in Cl_2 is 0. In Cl^- it is –1, which is a *decrease* in oxidation number and is therefore a *reduction*. In ClO^-, the oxidation number of the chlorine is +1 (check it yourself). This is an *increase* in oxidation number and is therefore an *oxidation*. So the chlorine has been both oxidised and reduced.

Following the rules of Stock notation, the ClO^- ion is called the chlorate(I) ion.

The reaction of chlorine with hot sodium hydroxide

$$3Cl_2(aq) + 6OH^-(aq) \rightarrow 5Cl^-(aq) + ClO_3^-(aq) + 3H_2O(l)$$

In this reaction, further oxidation takes place to produce ClO_3^- ions. Using Stock notation, the ClO_3^- ion is called chlorate(V).

The reaction of iodine with sodium hydroxide

$$3I_2(aq) + 6OH^-(aq) \longrightarrow 5I^-(aq) + IO_3^-(aq) + 3H_2O(l)$$

Tip Remember that in a disproportionation reaction the oxidation number of one of the elements will both increase and decrease.

The reaction of iodine with sodium thiosulphate

This is an important redox reaction used in titrations to measure the amount of iodine present in a solution:

$$2S_2O_3^{2-}(aq) + I_2(aq) \longrightarrow 2I^-(aq) + S_4O_6^{2-}(aq)$$

An aqueous iodine solution (in a conical flask) is titrated with sodium thiosulphate, $Na_2S_2O_3$ (in a burette), using starch as the indicator. As the titration proceeds, the orange colour due to the iodine gradually becomes pale yellow. A very pale yellow solution turning colourless would be a difficult end point to see, so near the end point two or three drops of starch are added so that the solution immediately turns an intense blue/black colour. The end point is when this becomes colourless, which is easy to see.

Chemical properties of halide anions

The halide anions chloride, bromide and iodide (Cl^-, Br^- and I^- respectively) are the ions formed from halogen atoms by gaining one electron (reduction). They all have the oxidation number −1 and are commonly used as the sodium or potassium salts.

Reaction with aqueous silver ions (silver nitrate solution)

The reactions of halide anions with aqueous silver ions are the tests for the halide anions.

Halide anion	Equation	Appearance of product	Solubility of product in ammonia solution
Cl^-	$Ag^+(aq) + Cl^-(aq) \longrightarrow AgCl(s)$	White precipitate, which darkens in sunlight	Soluble in dilute solution
Br^-	$Ag^+(aq) + Br^-(aq) \longrightarrow AgBr(s)$	Cream precipitate, which darkens in sunlight	Soluble in concentrated solution
I^-	$Ag^+(aq) + I^-(aq) \longrightarrow AgI(s)$	Yellow precipitate	Insoluble, even in concentrated solution

Tip It might look a lot to learn, but try to recognise the patterns and trends in the behaviour of the ions. In the equations, the spectator ions (sodium or potassium and nitrate) have been left out. Pay careful attention to the state symbols.

Reaction with concentrated sulphuric acid

The idea is to use the reaction of solid sodium (or potassium) halides with concentrated sulphuric acid to prepare pure samples of the hydrogen halides. It doesn't work!

Solid halide	Appearance of product	Equation
KCl	White, misty fumes (of HCl)	KCl(s) + H2SO4(l) › KHSO4(s) + HCl(g)
KBr	White, misty fumes (of HBr)	KBr(s) + H2SO4(l) › KHSO4(s) + HBr(g)
	Mixture turns orange (owing to the presence of bromine)	$2HBr(g) + H_2SO_4(l) \longrightarrow Br_2(aq) + SO_2(g) + 2H_2O(l)$
KI	A real mess! Mixture goes black because of the production of iodine; SO_2 and H_2S can be detected; yellow solid may appear (sulphur)	

With the possible exception of HCl, this is not a good way of making hydrogen halides. However, there is a lot of chemistry going on. The problem is that concentrated sulphuric acid is a powerful oxidising agent. Hydrogen bromide is quite a strong reducing agent, so as soon as it is produced, it starts to react with the sulphuric acid to produce bromine (orange) and sulphur dioxide. Therefore, not much hydrogen bromide is left.

The real fun begins in the reaction with potassium iodide. Hydrogen iodide is a strong reducer. As soon as it is produced it reacts vigorously with the sulphuric acid. The hydrogen iodide is oxidised to iodine and the sulphuric acid is reduced to sulphur dioxide, sulphur and even to hydrogen sulphide. (Check the oxidation number changes for the sulphur — it goes from +6 all the way down to −2.) There is virtually no hydrogen iodide product.

As a result of carrying out these redox reactions, the examiners expect you to know how to test for sulphur dioxide and hydrogen sulphide.

Gas	Test	Positive result
Sulphur dioxide, SO_2	Filter paper strip soaked in a mixture of dilute sulphuric acid and potassium dichromate	Colour change from orange to green
Hydrogen sulphide, H_2S	Filter paper strip soaked in lead nitrate (or ethanoate) solution	Colour change from colourless to black

Reaction with concentrated phosphoric acid

Concentrated phosphoric acid is used to make pure samples of the hydrogen halide gases. Like sulphuric acid, it is a strong acid. However, it is not a powerful oxidiser.

Solid halide	Equation	Appearance of product
KCl	$3KCl(s) + H_3PO_4(l) \rightarrow K_3PO_4(aq) + 3HCl(g)$	White, misty fumes
KBr	$3KBr(s) + H_3PO_4(l) \rightarrow K_3PO_4(aq) + 3HBr(g)$	White, misty fumes
KI	$3KI(s) + H_3PO_4(l) \rightarrow K_3PO_4(aq) + 3HI(g)$	White, misty fumes

Because phosphoric acid is not a powerful oxidiser there are no side redox reactions with the hydrogen halide products, and these can be collected in a relatively pure state. The apparatus used for this preparation is simple:

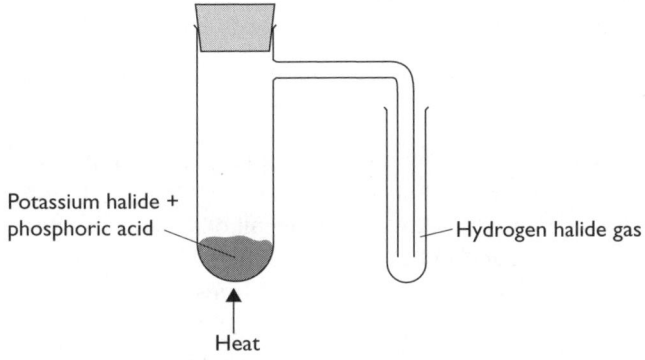

Chemical properties of the hydrogen halides

There are three properties that you need to know:
- Solubility in water — immerse a test tube of the gas under water and see how far the water rises up the tube. If the tube is initially full of gas, the water should rise all the way up the tube.
- Reaction with ammonia gas should give a white smoky vapour of the ammonium halide.
- Thermal stability — plunge a red-hot nichrome wire or spatula end into a test tube of the gas and look for the colour of the halogen element being produced (see table).

Hydrogen halide	Solubility in water	Reaction with ammonia gas	Thermal stability
HCl	Very soluble	Dense, white fumes $HCl(g) + NH_3(g) \rightarrow NH_4Cl(s)$	No reaction Thermally stable
HBr	Very soluble	Dense, white fumes $HBr(g) + NH_3(g) \rightarrow NH_4Br(s)$	Some orange vapour $2HBr(g) \rightarrow H_2(g) + Br_2(g)$
HI	Very soluble	Dense, white fumes $HI(g) + NH_3(g) \rightarrow NH_4I(s)$	Clouds of purple vapour $2HI(g) \rightarrow H_2(g) + I_2(g)$

In summary:
- The hydrogen halide gases are all very soluble in water.
- They all react with ammonia gas, producing dense white fumes.

- Their thermal stability *decreases* as the group is descended. Hydrogen chloride does not decompose on heating, hydrogen bromide undergoes some **thermal decomposition** and hydrogen iodide readily undergoes thermal decomposition to produce clouds of iodine vapour.

Covalency

- Simple covalent substances consist of *molecules* (not ions).
- Covalent bonds consist of pairs of electrons *shared* between the atoms.

Dot-and-cross diagrams are used to illustrate the covalent bonding/electron sharing between atoms.

These are simple diagrams that nevertheless require care and thought, as it is all too easy to leave electrons out. Generally, only the outer electrons are shown, but occasionally the examiner will ask you to show all of them. Make sure that you read the question to establish exactly what is required. Remember that electrons are shared in pairs and that most atoms will have eight electrons around them (four pairs).

$$H \overset{\times\times}{\underset{\times\times}{\overset{\times}{\text{Cl}}\times}} \qquad \overset{\times\times}{\underset{\times\times}{\overset{\times}{\text{Cl}}\times}} \overset{\cdot\cdot}{\underset{\cdot\cdot}{\overset{\cdot}{\text{Cl}}\cdot}}$$

Shapes of molecules

The shapes of molecules can be worked out from dot-and-cross diagrams by looking at the arrangement of the electrons around the central atom. You have to consider electrons in two different situations:
- those pairs that are involved in the bonding between two atoms — **bonding pairs**
- those pairs that are *not* involved in the bonding between two atoms — **lone pairs**

Electron pairs repel each other, so that they are as far away from each other as possible. This ensures the maximum stability for the structure.
- Bonding pairs repel bonding pairs *quite* strongly.
- Lone pairs repel bonding pairs *more* strongly.
- Lone pairs repel lone pairs *most* strongly.

This is known as the **electron-pair repulsion theory**.

In beryllium chloride, boron trifluoride and methane, only bonding pairs are involved. Electron-pair repulsion results in molecules with the following shapes:

Cl—Be—Cl 180° Linear

F—B with F, F 120° Planar

C with 4 H 109.5° Tetrahedral

In ammonia and water there is the added complication of lone pairs. In both cases, there are four pairs of electrons around the central atom, so the arrangement of the electron pairs will be tetrahedral, as in methane. However, a lone pair exerts a greater repulsion on the bonding pairs and consequently the bonds are squeezed closer together. This is why the bond angle in ammonia is *not* 109.5° but is reduced slightly to 107°. In water, the two lone pairs repel each other strongly and push the bonding pairs even closer — hence the smaller angle of 104.5°.

Name	Formula	Number of electron pairs involved	Shape	Bond angle
Beryllium chloride	$BeCl_2$	2 bonding pairs	Linear	180°
Boron trifluoride	BF_3	3 bonding pairs	Planar	120°
Methane	CH_4	4 bonding pairs	Tetrahedral	109.5°
Ammonia	NH_3	3 bonding pairs; 1 lone pair	Pyramidal	107°
Water	H_2O	2 bonding pairs; 2 lone pairs	Bent	104.5°

Tip It is a good idea to learn the shapes of the molecules and the bond angles. Guesswork will not help and could result in you suggesting something silly, like water molecules being linear. Sometimes the examiner will try to fool you with an unfamiliar molecule. For example, you could be asked about the bond angle around the oxygen in an alcohol. This is just like the oxygen in water and the angle is 104.5°. Look for bonding pairs *and* lone pairs to help work out the bond angle.

Multiple bonds

A double bond consists of two pairs of electrons, but it is not the equivalent of two single bonds. One of the bonds is as strong as a single bond and is called a **sigma**-bond (σ-bond). The other component is weaker and is known as a **pi**-bond (π-bond). In ethane, C_2H_6, the σ-bond electron pair occupies the space directly between the two carbon atom nuclei. The π-bond electron pair occupies spaces above and below this:

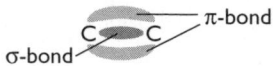

Giant covalent structures

It is not just simple molecules such as carbon dioxide and water in which the atoms are joined to each other by covalent bonds. There are some non-metal substances in which atoms are joined together by covalent bonds to form giant lattice structures containing billions of atoms. These include diamond and graphite (both consisting of carbon *atoms*) and silicon dioxide (consisting of millions of silicon dioxide *molecules*).

Diamond
In diamond, each carbon atom is joined by covalent bonds to *four* other carbon atoms, giving rise to a strong tetrahedral structure.

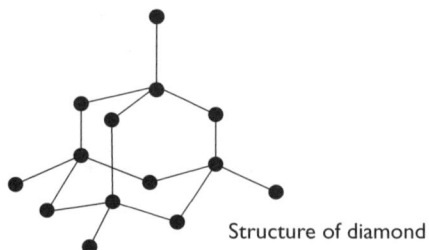

Structure of diamond

All four of the outer electrons are involved in the bonding. Therefore, diamond:
- does not conduct electricity
- is very hard
- has extremely high melting and boiling points

Graphite

In graphite, each carbon atom is joined to *three* other carbon atoms by covalent bonds. The carbon atoms are arranged in hexagonal rings (of six carbon atoms) and these rings are joined to each other to form layers.

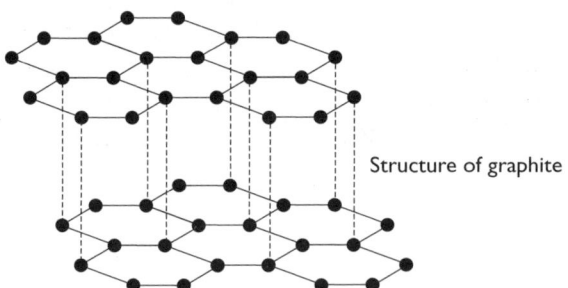

Structure of graphite

The covalent bonding *within* the layers is very strong, so graphite has high melting and boiling points. The bonding *between* the layers is weak and the layers can move over each other easily. This makes graphite a very soft material and useful in lubricants and as the 'lead' in pencils.

Since each carbon atom forms only three bonds, only three of the four outer electrons are involved in covalent bonding. The fourth electron is free to move and belongs to the whole structure. Such electrons are said to be **delocalised**. It is because of these delocalised electrons that graphite can conduct electricity.

Dative covalency

There is no chemical or physical difference between an ordinary covalent bond and a dative covalent bond.
- In an ordinary covalent bond formed by the sharing of a pair of electrons by two atoms, each atom contributes one electron to the pair.
- In a dative covalent bond, both the electrons in the pair are contributed by one of the atoms. The other atom does not contribute any electrons. Atoms capable of

doing this have a lone pair, for example the oxygen in water and the nitrogen in ammonia. Both ammonia and water can form dative covalent bonds, for example with hydrogen ions.

$H_2O: + H^+ \longrightarrow H_3O^+$
$:NH_3 + H^+ \longrightarrow NH_4^+$

Once a lone pair has been used in bonding to another atom, the shape of the resulting ion is different. The ammonium ion, NH_4^+, has just the four bonding pairs and so the shape is tetrahedral and the bond angle is 109.5°. In the hydroxonium ion, H_3O^+, there are now three bonding pairs and one lone pair, just like in ammonia, so the bond angle is 107°.

Ammonium ion   Hydroxonium ion

Dative covalent bonds also occur in nitric acid and carbon monoxide:

Nitric acid   Carbon monoxide

Tip You should practise drawing these structures.

Electronegativity

The **electronegativity** of an atom is its ability to attract the electrons *in a covalent bond*. (The words in italics are often forgotten!)

Tip Electronegativity is not the answer to everything. You must be careful how you use this concept. For a start, you cannot have electronegative ions, molecules or bonds. The idea of electronegativity applies *only* to atoms in a molecule. Learn the definition.

There are several systems that attempt to give numerical values to the electronegativity of atoms. However, none is really satisfactory. All you need to know is that elements become more electronegative:
- on moving across a period from left to right
- on ascending a group

The most electronegative element is fluorine, followed by oxygen and then nitrogen.

Polarity

In hydrogen chloride, the chlorine is more electronegative than the hydrogen. Therefore, it attracts the *bonding* electrons to itself. This means that the bonding electrons are not shared equally. They spend more time orbiting the chlorine. This means that the chlorine is more negative than the hydrogen and the bond is **polarised**.

$$H^{\delta+}:Cl^{\delta-}$$

- The δ+ sign on the hydrogen atom shows that it has a partial positive charge.
- The δ− sign on the chlorine atom shows that it has a partial negative charge.

The electrons are still shared; it is just that they are not shared equally. The bond is **polar** and has some ionic character. This is common in molecules that contain an electronegative atom.

Remember that the electronegativities of carbon and hydrogen are almost equal and so carbon–hydrogen bonds are *not* polar. The bonding electrons are shared equally and compounds such as methane, ethane and ethene are not polar.

Molecules such as water, ammonia, hydrogen fluoride and ethanol contain very electronegative atoms and thus have polar bonds. The molecules themselves are polar and are said to possess a **dipole**.

Bond breaking

Bond energies and enthalpies of reaction

Standard enthalpy change of combustion, $\Delta H_c^\ominus$

This is the enthalpy change when 1 mole of substance undergoes complete combustion under standard conditions.

Experimentally determined values of $\Delta H_c^\ominus$ can be used to calculate $\Delta H_f^\ominus$ using Hess's law; for example, for methane, CH_4:

$$C(s) + 2H_2(g) \longrightarrow CH_4(g)$$

$\Delta H_f^\ominus(CO_2(g)) = -393.5 \text{ kJ mol}^{-1}$
$2 \times \Delta H_f^\ominus(H_2O(l)) = 2 \times -285.8 \text{ kJ mol}^{-1}$

$\Delta H_c^\ominus(CH_4(g)) = -890.3 \text{ kJ mol}^{-1}$

$$CO_2(g) + 2H_2O(l)$$

Using Hess's law,

$\Delta H_f^\ominus(CH_4(g)) + (-890.3) = -393.5 + 2(-285.8)$

Therefore,

$\Delta H_f^\ominus(CH_4(g)) = -74.8 \text{ kJ mol}^{-1}$

Finding values of $\Delta H_f^\ominus$ is the first step towards determining individual bond energies. However, you also need to know some atomisation enthalpy values.

Standard enthalpy of atomisation, $\Delta H^\ominus_{at}$

This is the enthalpy change when 1 mole of gaseous atoms is made from an element in its standard state under standard conditions. For example:

$C(s) \longrightarrow C(g)$ $\Delta H^\ominus_{at}(C(s)) = +716.7 \text{ kJ mol}^{-1}$

$\frac{1}{2}H_2(g) \longrightarrow H(g)$ $\Delta H^\ominus_{at}(H(g)) = +218 \text{ kJ mol}^{-1}$

Values of $\Delta H^\ominus_{at}$ are always positive because bonds are broken to produce individual atoms and this requires energy.

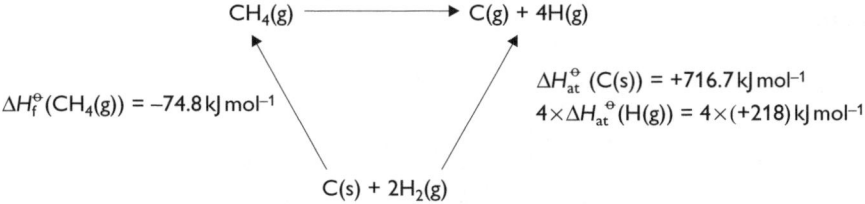

$\Delta H^\ominus_{at}(H(g))$ is multiplied by 4 because 4 moles of hydrogen atoms are made; $\Delta H^\ominus_{at}$ is per mole of atoms formed.

Using Hess's law to find $\Delta H^\ominus_{at}(CH_4(g))$:

$\Delta H^\ominus_f(CH_4(g)) + \Delta H^\ominus_{at}(CH_4(g)) = \Delta H^\ominus_{at}(C(g)) + 4 \times \Delta H^\ominus_{at}(H(g))$

$-74.8 + \Delta H^\ominus_{at}(CH_4(g)) = +716.7 + (4 \times 218)$

$\Delta H^\ominus_{at}(CH_4(g)) = 74.8 + 716.7 + 872 = +1663.5 \text{ kJ mol}^{-1}$

This is the amount of energy required to break up 1 mole of methane molecules into its individual atoms — in other words, the energy needed to break 4 moles of C–H bonds. Therefore, the energy required to break 1 mole of C–H bonds is one-quarter of this, or $+416 \text{ kJ mol}^{-1}$. This is the bond energy of the C–H bond, which is written as $E(\text{C–H})$.

There are several points to remember about bond energies:
- They are always positive because energy is needed to break bonds. Bond energy is the amount of energy that has to be put in to break the bond.
- Bond energies are only average values. Calculations involving them give approximate values. (This is popular with examiners.)
- Bond energies vary according to the type of molecule. For instance, $E(\text{C–Cl})$ in CCl_4 is $+327 \text{ kJ mol}^{-1}$; $E(\text{C–Cl})$ in C_2H_5Cl is $+342 \text{ kJ mol}^{-1}$.
- Between any two atoms, a double bond will have higher bond energy than a single bond (it will also be shorter). A triple bond will have even more energy. This is because there are more electrons in the space between the nuclei, pulling the nuclei towards each other.

Bond	Bond energy/kJ mol^{-1}	Bond length/nm
C–N	286	0.147
C=N	615	0.130
C≡N	887	0.116

Bond energies and rates of reaction

Reactions occur only when the reacting particles collide. However, collision alone is not enough. They must collide with sufficient energy to break bonds. The greater the bond energy involved, the more energetic the collision must be.

Sometimes new bonds start to form before the old ones have finished breaking. This gives rise to a **transition state** that is half-way between the original reacting molecules and the new molecules being formed. The transition state represents a position of **maximum energy**.

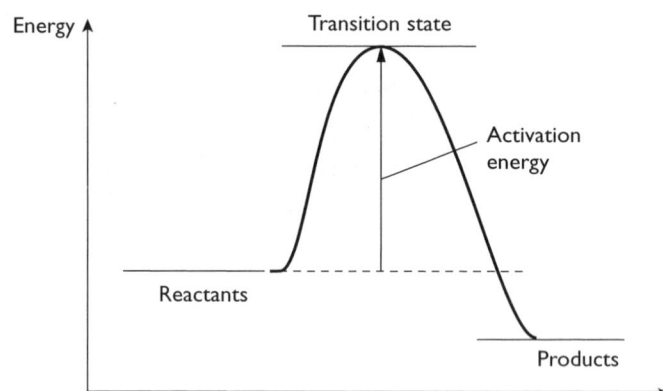

- The difference between the energy of the reactants and the energy of the transition state is the **activation energy**, E_a. To be successful, a collision between two particles must have energy equal to, or greater than, the activation energy.
- The greater the bond energies of the bonds to be broken, the greater the activation energy and the slower the reaction will be.
- Increasing the temperature increases the kinetic energy of the particles and thus the energy of the collisions. This causes more collisions per second, but much more importantly, more collisions will have energy equal to or greater than the activation energy, so the reaction will be faster.

Catalysis

A catalyst speeds up a reaction by providing an alternative route (or mechanism) that has a lower activation energy and a different transition state.

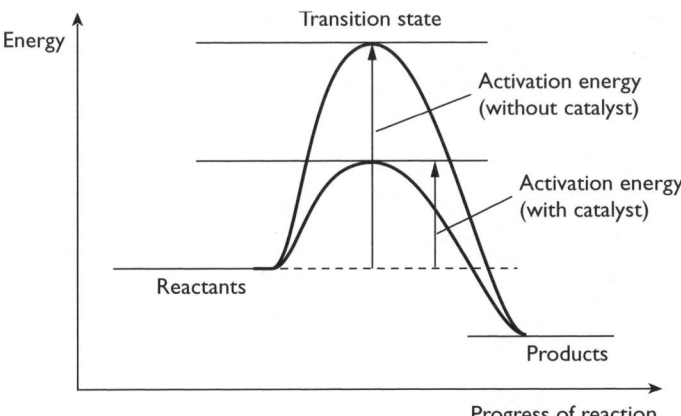

Tip A catalyst does *not* 'lower the activation energy'. This is a common answer, which is always marked wrong by the examiner.

Reversible reactions

Reversible reactions can occur in either direction. There are many reactions that can go in both directions at the same time. When a reaction goes in the forward and the reverse direction at the same time and *at the same rate* it is in **dynamic equilibrium**. One example is the manufacture of ammonia by the Haber process:

$$N_2(g) + 3H_2(g) \rightleftharpoons 2NH_3(g)$$

When this reaction reaches equilibrium, every time two molecules of ammonia are formed, two molecules of ammonia are broken down and the concentration of all the substances *stays the same*.

At equilibrium:
- there is no change in the concentrations of the reactants or the products; this does *not* mean that the reaction has stopped
- both the forward and reverse reactions are taking place simultaneously, at the same rate

Equilibrium can be achieved by starting with either the reactants or the products.

Le Chatelier's principle

Le Chatelier's principle states: 'If the conditions under which an equilibrium exists are changed, the position of equilibrium alters in such a way as to tend to oppose the change in conditions.' More simply, whenever there is a change in the conditions of a reaction at equilibrium, the position of equilibrium shifts in the direction that opposes the change.

This useful idea enables you to predict what will happen to a reaction at equilibrium if the conditions are changed.

Change in concentration

In the Haber process, an increase in the concentration of nitrogen means that the equilibrium will adjust to decrease the concentration of nitrogen.

$$N_2(g) + 3H_2(g) \rightleftharpoons 2NH_3(g)$$

The equilibrium position will shift to the right and more ammonia will be formed. Eventually, the reaction will reach equilibrium again, but now the mixture will contain a greater concentration of ammonia.

Change in pressure

If the pressure is increased, the equilibrium position will shift in the direction that reduces the pressure.

$$N_2(g) + 3H_2(g) \rightleftharpoons 2NH_3(g)$$

The side of the reaction with fewer molecules exerts a lower pressure. In this case, the 2 moles on the right-hand side of the equation exert a lower pressure than the 4 moles on the left-hand side of the equation. On increasing the pressure, the equilibrium will shift towards the right-hand side and more ammonia will be produced. Decreasing the pressure would have the opposite effect.

Beware the situation where the number of moles is the same on *both* sides of the equation. For example:

$$H_2(g) + Br_2(g) \rightleftharpoons 2HBr(g)$$

Here, changing the pressure will have *no effect* on the equilibrium.

Change in temperature

To be able to predict the effect of a change in temperature you need to know whether the forward reaction is exothermic or endothermic. Values of ΔH quoted for equilibrium reactions always refer to the forward reaction. The numerical value for the reverse reaction will be the same but the sign will be opposite.

For the Haber process, $\Delta H^\ominus = -92 \text{ kJ mol}^{-1}$, so the forward reaction is exothermic. If the temperature is increased, the equilibrium will shift in the direction that decreases the temperature, that is, the endothermic direction. In this case, the amount of ammonia in the equilibrium mixture will decrease.
- Putting heat energy into a reversible reaction favours the endothermic direction.
- Taking heat energy from a reversible reaction (by cooling) favours the exothermic direction.

Effect of adding a catalyst

The presence of a catalyst does not affect the *position* of equilibrium. However, it does mean that a reversible reaction will reach equilibrium more quickly. This is because the catalyst speeds up both the forward and the reverse reactions equally — so one side of the equation is not favoured over the other.

Tip Watch out for this one, it's a common trap!

Hydrocarbons

Alkanes

Alkanes are hydrocarbons (compounds that contain carbon and hydrogen only). They constitute a homologous series of general formula C_nH_{2n+2}. You need to learn the names of the alkanes that have straight-chain molecules. The first four in the series are:

- methane — CH_4
- ethane — C_2H_6
- propane — C_3H_8
- butane — C_4H_{10}

Alkane molecules can also be branched; this gives rise to **structural isomerism**. Structural isomers are compounds with the same molecular formula but different structural formulae. For example:

H_3C——CH_2——CH_2——CH_3
Butane

$$H_3C-\underset{\underset{CH_3}{|}}{CH}-CH_3$$
2-methylpropane

To name a branched structure such as:

$$H_3C-\underset{\underset{CH_3}{|}}{CH}-\underset{\underset{CH_3}{|}}{CH}-CH_2-CH_3$$

- start with the longest continuous chain of carbon atoms. Here, the longest chain is five carbon atoms, so it is a pentane chain.
- identify the branches. Here, they both have single carbon atoms, so they are both methyl groups.
- identify the numbers of the carbon atoms on the pentane chain to which the branches are attached. Choose the lowest combination. Here, the branches are attached to the second and third carbon atoms. It is '2,3' rather than '3,4' because 2,3 is the lower combination.

Therefore, this molecule is 2,3-dimethylpentane. It is called **di**methyl because there are two methyl groups. The molecular formula is C_7H_{16}, so 2,3-dimethylpentane is an isomer of heptane.

The formulae above are **structural** formulae. Remember the difference between a structural formula and a **displayed** formula, which shows *all the atoms and all the bonds*.

Tip Do not mix up structural and displayed formulae. Always read the question carefully to see what the examiner is asking for.

Cyclohexane, C_6H_{12}, is an example of a cyclic alkane. The structural formula is often drawn as a simplified skeletal formula.

Structural formula   Simplified skeletal formula

Cyclohexane is not an isomer of hexane because it does not have the same molecular formula.

Reactions of alkanes

The values of the bond energies, $E(C-C)$ and $E(C-H)$, are high. This makes alkanes unreactive. They do not react with oxidising agents, *aqueous* solutions of halogens, concentrated sulphuric acid or alkalis.

Combustion

In a plentiful supply of air, alkanes burn with a clean flame (which shows a low carbon-to-hydrogen ratio). The combustion produces a lot of energy. These two factors are the reasons why the main use of alkanes is as fuels. The **complete combustion** of an alkane produces carbon dioxide and water. For example, for propane:

$$C_3H_8(g) + 5O_2(g) \longrightarrow 3CO_2(g) + 4H_2O(l) \quad \Delta H^\ominus = -2219.2 \text{ kJ mol}^{-1}$$

In a poor supply of oxygen, **incomplete combustion** occurs. Toxic carbon monoxide is produced:

$$C_3H_8(g) + \tfrac{7}{2}O_2(g) \longrightarrow 3CO(g) + 4H_2O(l) \quad \Delta H^\ominus = -1370.2 \text{ kJ mol}^{-1}$$

Tip Always use the term 'toxic'. Do not use 'dangerous' or 'harmful'. These words are not specific enough.

Cracking

Cracking describes the breaking up by heat of large alkane molecules that are in plentiful supply (but for which there is a low demand) into smaller molecules (for which there is a great demand but insufficient supply).

The apparatus used in the laboratory is shown below:

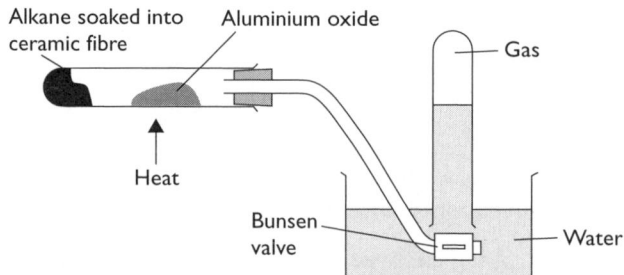

Some practical points are:
- The aluminium oxide catalyst is heated.
- The first test tube of gas is discarded because it contains mainly air from the apparatus.
- A Bunsen valve is used to avoid the danger of sucking back cold water into the hot reaction tube.

Industrially, a silica–alumina catalyst is used.

A typical equation is:
$$C_{10}H_{22}(g) \rightarrow C_8H_{18}(g) + C_2H_4(g)$$

The alkane C_8H_{18} (octane) is used in petrol and $C_2H_4(g)$ (ethene) is an extremely useful alkene.

Reaction of alkanes with halogens in ultraviolet light

Using methane as an example, the overall reaction is:
$$CH_4(g) + Cl_2(g) \rightarrow CH_3Cl(l) + HCl(g)$$

This is a **substitution** reaction because one atom in a molecule is being replaced by a different atom.

The mechanism of the reaction is in three stages:
- **Chain initiation** — this is a **photochemical** reaction because ultraviolet (UV) light is an essential condition. The UV light provides the energy to split chlorine molecules into atoms:
$$Cl_2 \rightarrow 2Cl\bullet$$

The bond has been broken (**fission**). Each of the chlorine atoms produced possesses one of the shared electrons that originally made up the covalent bond between the chlorine atoms. This is called **homolytic fission**. The products of homolytic fission always have one unpaired electron and are called **free radicals**. Free radicals are extremely reactive.

- **Chain propagation** — the chlorine free radicals start a chain reaction:
$$Cl\bullet + CH_4 \rightarrow CH_3\bullet + HCl$$
$$CH_3\bullet + Cl_2 \rightarrow CH_3Cl + Cl\bullet$$

- **Chain termination** — when the concentrations of chlorine and methane fall, the free radicals tend to react with each other:
$$Cl\bullet + Cl\bullet \rightarrow Cl_2$$
$$Cl\bullet + CH_3\bullet \rightarrow CH_3Cl$$
$$CH_3\bullet + CH_3\bullet \rightarrow C_2H_6$$

The main overall reaction is a substitution because one atom (a chlorine) replaces another atom (hydrogen) in methane. The reagent is a free radical, so this reaction is an example of a **free-radical substitution**.

Other reactions involving free radicals are the combustion reactions of alkanes above and the polymerisation of alkenes.

Note that if the fission were **heterolytic**, one of the chlorine atoms would possess both of the original shared electrons and the other chlorine atom would have none:

$$Cl_2 \longrightarrow Cl^+ + Cl^-$$

This kind of fission requires more energy than UV light can provide.

Alkenes

The alkenes are a homologous series of general formula C_nH_{2n}.

The first three members are:
- ethene — C_2H_4
- propene — C_3H_6
- butene — C_4H_8

The important thing to remember is that alkenes are **unsaturated** molecules. This means that they have a double bond between two of the carbon atoms. For example:

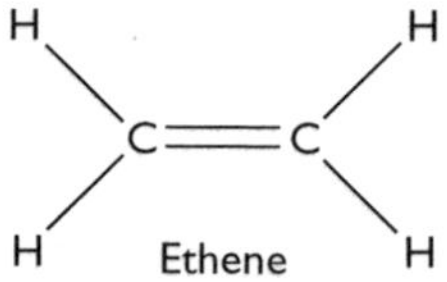

Ethene

Butene is the first member of the series to have isomers. The position of the double bond can vary and there is also a branched isomer:

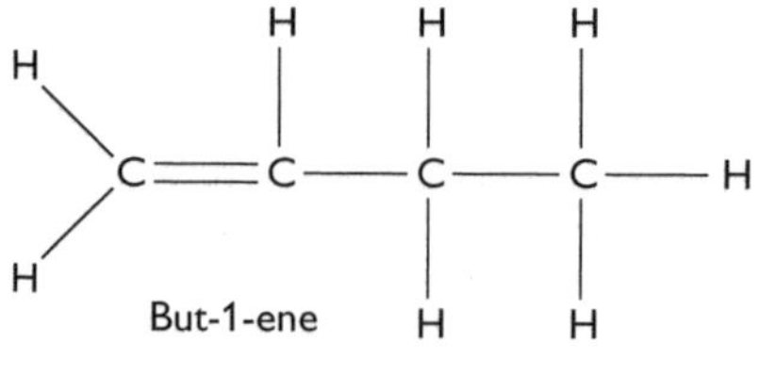

But-1-ene 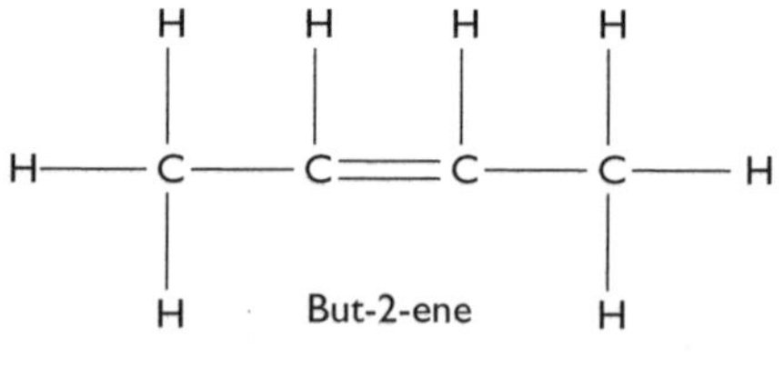   But-2-ene

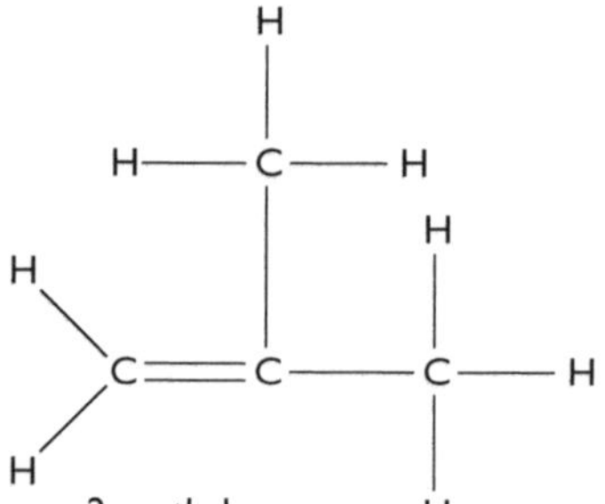

2-methylpropene

There is free rotation about a single bond but there is no free rotation about a double bond. This means that the groups on the double-bonded carbon atoms are fixed, giving rise to **geometric isomers**:

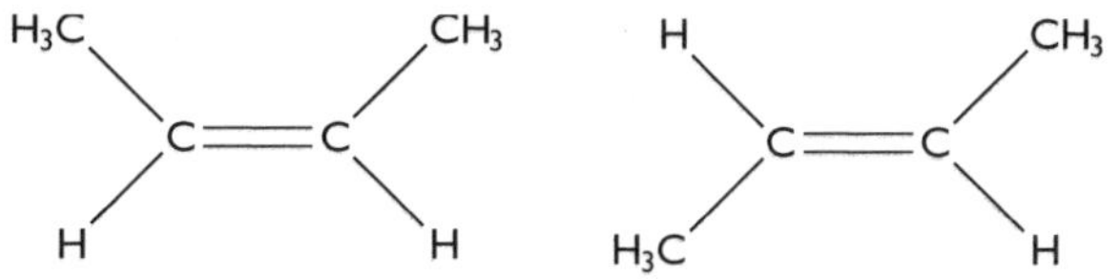

cis-but-2-ene   trans-but-2-ene

There is no free rotation about a carbon–carbon double bond because of the arrangement of the electron clouds making up the bond. There is a sigma-bond (σ-bond) joining the centres of the atoms and a pi-bond (π-bond) above and below the molecule. For rotation to occur, the π-bond would have to be broken. This requires energy, so it does not happen.

Reactions of alkenes

The π-bond (+264 kJ mol^{-1}) is weaker than the σ-bond (+346 kJ mol^{-1}) and is easier to break. This makes alkenes more reactive than alkanes.

Combustion

Alkenes are highly flammable, burning with a slightly sooty, yellow flame. The soot indicates a higher carbon-to-hydrogen ratio than in alkanes.

Oxidation

Alkenes readily change the colour of potassium manganate(VII) in sulphuric acid from purple to colourless. The alkene is oxidised to a diol. For example:

$$CH_2=CH_2 + KMnO_4 \longrightarrow CH_2OHCH_2OH$$
  Ethene   Ethane-1,2-diol

Action of bromine

This is a test for unsaturation. Alkenes instantly turn an aqueous solution of bromine from orange to colourless.

The attacking species in this reaction is a polarised bromine molecule, Br$^{\delta+}$–Br$^{\delta-}$. As this approaches the electron-rich double bond of an ethene molecule, the π-bond starts to break and the two electrons begin to form a new bond to the Br$^{\delta+}$:

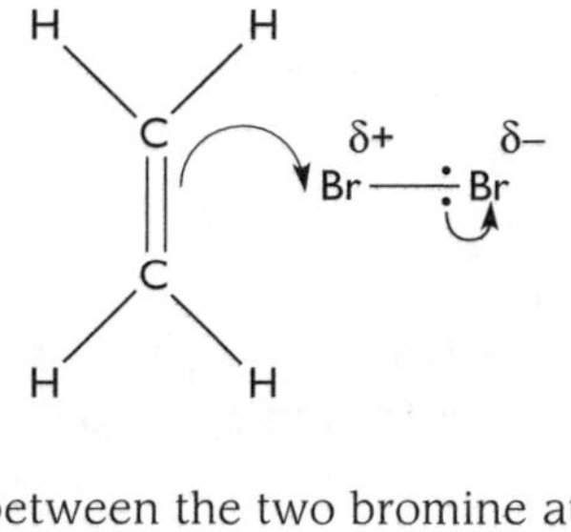

As this happens, the bond between the two bromine atoms also starts to break. This leads to the formation of an unstable intermediate ion (a **carbocation**) and a bromide anion:

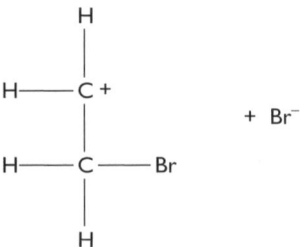

The reaction is completed by the bromide anion using a pair of its electrons to form a new bond to the positively charged carbon atom:

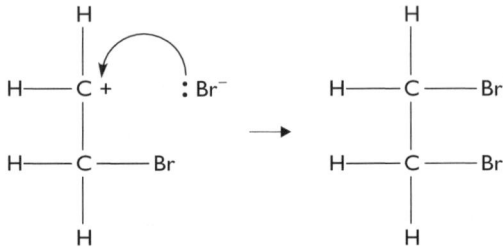

Two reactants have joined together to form one molecule (1,2-dibromoethane), so this is an **addition** reaction. The initial attack is by $Br^{\delta+}$, which is an **electrophile**. Therefore, this is an example of an **electrophilic addition** reaction.

An electrophile is an electron-deficient species (usually with a full or partial positive charge) *that can form a new covalent bond using a pair of electrons from the carbon compound*. Alkenes typically undergo electrophilic addition reactions.

Action of concentrated sulphuric acid
This is another electrophilic addition reaction. The electrophile is H^+ from the sulphuric acid. Using ethene as an example, the product is ethyl hydrogen sulphate:

$CH_2=CH_2 + H_2SO_4 \longrightarrow CH_3-CH_2SO_4H$

Ethyl hydrogen sulphate can be reacted with water to produce ethanol:

$CH_3CH_2SO_4H + H_2O \longrightarrow C_2H_5OH + H_2SO_4$

This is a **hydrolysis** reaction because ethyl hydrogen sulphate is being split up by water.

Polymerisation
Polymerisation is the joining together of many small molecules (monomers) to form one long, giant chain (the polymer). When ethene is the monomer, the polymer formed is poly(ethene). This is an example of **addition polymerisation** — the monomer molecules add to each other to form the polymer as the only product:

$nCH_2=CH_2 \longrightarrow \text{\textendash}[CH_2-CH_2]_n\text{\textendash}$

Peroxides are used to produce free radicals, which start the reaction.

Uses of hydrocarbons

Alkanes
The principal uses are:
- fuels (domestic, petrol and diesel)
- lubricating oils
- feedstock for the petrochemical industry to make industrially important chemicals such as benzene, ethanoic acid and ethene

Alkenes
The principal uses are:
- making polymers such as poly(ethene), poly(phenylethene) and poly(chloroethene)
- making diols such as ethane-1,2-diol
- making ethanol

Halogenoalkanes

Halogenoalkanes are molecules formed when halogen atoms replace hydrogen atoms in alkanes. For example:
- bromomethane — CH_3Br
- iodoethane — C_2H_5I

The halogen atoms can occur on any of the carbon atoms in any part of a molecule, including branches. Halogenoalkanes are classified as **primary**, **secondary** or **tertiary** according to how many alkyl groups are attached to the carbon carrying the halogen atom.

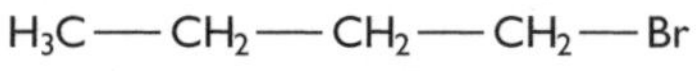

$H_3C-CH_2-CH_2-CH_2-Br$

1-bromobutane
(primary — one group)

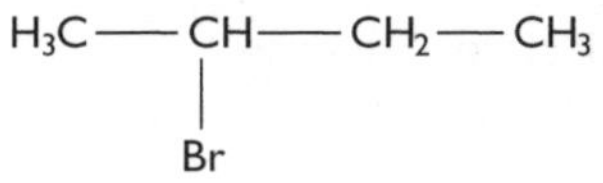

$H_3C-CH(Br)-CH_2-CH_3$

2-bromobutane
(secondary — two groups)

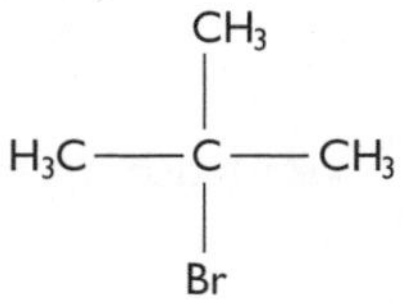

$H_3C-C(CH_3)(Br)-CH_3$

2-bromo-2-methylpropane
(tertiary — three groups)

There can also be more than one halogen atom in a molecule:

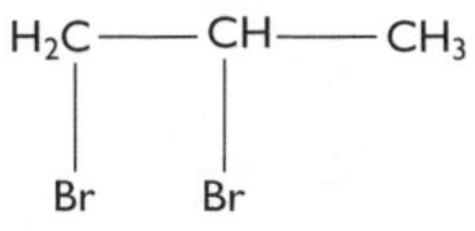

$H_2C(Br)-CH(Br)-CH_3$

1,2-dibromopropane

Reactions of halogenoalkanes

Combustion
Halogenoalkanes are flammable and burn with a clean, yellow flame.

Reaction with aqueous alkali

This is a **substitution** reaction — the halogen atom in the molecule is replaced by an –OH group. For example:

$$C_2H_5Br + OH^- \longrightarrow C_2H_5OH + Br^-$$

Although the reagent is called 'aqueous alkali', the alkali is actually dissolved in a mixture of water and ethanol. The halogenoalkane would not dissolve much if water alone were used as the solvent.

The attacking species is the OH⁻ ion, which has an unshared pair of electrons available to form a new covalent bond with the carbon atom.

Attacking groups that have an unshared pair of electrons available to form new covalent bonds are called **nucleophiles**. Therefore, this reaction is an example of **nucleophilic substitution**.

Reaction with alcoholic alkali

The reagent used is a hot, concentrated solution of potassium hydroxide dissolved in ethanol. In this reaction, the OH⁻ ion is acting *not* as a nucleophile but as a base. When ethanol alone is used as the solvent, the reaction is an **elimination** reaction and a double bond is introduced into the molecule.

$$(CH_3)_3C-Br + OH^- \longrightarrow (CH_3)_2C=CH_2 + H_2O + Br^-$$

Reaction with aqueous silver nitrate

This is a **nucleophilic substitution** reaction in which the nucleophile is water. The oxygen atom of a water molecule has an unshared electron pair available for bonding.

A typical equation is:

$$C_2H_5Br + H_2O \longrightarrow C_2H_5OH + H^+ + Br^- \quad \text{(slow)}$$

Tip This reaction could also be called hydrolysis because the molecule is being split using water.

In the presence of silver nitrate, a precipitate of the silver halide is formed:

$$Ag^+(aq) + Br^-(aq) \longrightarrow AgBr(s) \quad \text{(fast)}$$

The speed with which the precipitate is formed is an indication of how fast the nucleophilic substitution takes place and can be used to compare how quickly different halogenoalkanes react.

Halogenoalkane	Relative rate of hydrolysis	Carbon–halogen bond energy/kJ mol^{-1}	Carbon–halogen dipole moment/D
1-chlorobutane	Slow	351	2.16
1-bromobutane	Intermediate	293	1.93
1-iodobutane	Fast	234	1.88

These results suggest that the ease with which the halogenoalkane is hydrolysed depends on the bond energy rather than the strength of the dipole moment (measured in Debyes). The weaker the bond, the more easily broken it is.

The strength of the carbon–halogen bond varies according to whether it is in a primary, secondary or tertiary halogenoalkane.

Halogenoalkane	Type	Relative rate of hydrolysis	Carbon–halogen bond energy/kJ mol^{-1}
1-bromobutane	Primary	Slow	293
2-bromobutane	Secondary	Intermediate	284
2-bromo-2-methylpropane	Tertiary	Fast	263

The halogenoalkane with the weakest carbon–halogen bond is hydrolysed most rapidly.

Reaction with alcoholic ammonia

Ammonia acts as a nucleophile. It has an unshared pair of electrons with which it can form a new covalent bond with the carbon atom:

$$C_2H_5Br + :NH_3 \longrightarrow C_2H_5NH_2 + HBr$$

The bromine atom is replaced. Therefore, this is another example of a nucleophilic substitution reaction.
- Alcohol is used as the solvent. If water were used, then the halogenoalkane would be hydrolysed to the corresponding alcohol.
- Heat and pressure are needed to ensure a good yield.

Uses of halogenoalkanes

Halogenoalkane molecules are useful as:
- intermediates in the production of other substances, both in the laboratory and industrially, for example PVC production
- products in their own right, for example anaesthetics

Intermolecular forces

- Intermolecular forces are forces of attraction *between* molecules.
- Intramolecular forces are the covalent bonds that exist *within* molecules and hold the atoms to each other.
- Intermolecular forces are *weak*; intramolecular forces are *much stronger*.

Whatever type of particle a substance is made from, there will be forces pulling those particles towards each other. These forces of attraction are known as **cohesive** forces. There are three different types of such intermolecular forces:
- van der Waals forces (these are generally the weakest)
- permanent dipole attractions
- hydrogen bonds (these are generally the strongest)

All three types of intermolecular force are much weaker than the forces holding atoms together in a molecule and the forces that attract oppositely charged ions to each other in an ionic substance.

Van der Waals forces

Van der Waals forces are universal. They are present between all particles to some degree.

Even a simple atomic system such as helium requires energy to turn it from a solid into a gas:

$$He(s) \longrightarrow He(g)$$

This implies that there is some sort of 'bond' between the particles that has to be broken. Only a tiny amount of energy is needed for the conversion, so it must be a very weak 'bond'.

Consider the inert gas argon in its solid form. All the atoms are arranged in a regular, repeating pattern, touching each other. Each atom has 18 electrons that are in constant motion. At any given time, more of those electrons may be on one side of an atom than on the other. This means that one side of the atom will have a tiny positive charge ($\delta+$) and the other side a tiny negative charge ($\delta-$), that is, a tiny atomic dipole. This will affect the electron distribution in the neighbouring atoms. The $\delta+$ will attract electrons and the $\delta-$ will repel electrons. Therefore, each $\delta+$ will be next to a $\delta-$ and vice versa. Tiny attractions are set up between neighbouring atoms throughout the entire structure:

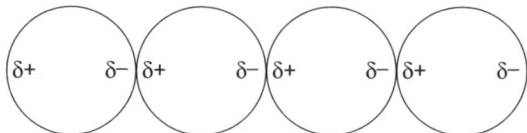

These electron dipoles are constantly fluctuating as the electrons move around the nucleus. However, they always do so together and therefore the forces of attraction are maintained.

Significance of van der Waals forces

Although van der Waals forces are extremely small, there are so many of them that they are important in determining how much energy is required to pull atoms away from each other so that the substance melts or boils.

The more electrons a substance has, the greater the van der Waals forces will be.

Substance	Number of electrons	Molar mass/g mol^{-1}	Boiling point/K
Helium	2	4	4
Neon	10	20	27
Argon	18	40	87
Krypton	36	84	121
Xenon	54	131	166

This applies to all substances and can be seen with the halogens and the alkanes. As the molecules get bigger, they have more electrons and thus greater van der Waals forces of attraction. Therefore, their boiling points increase because more energy is required to overcome the attractive forces.

The shape of a molecule is important too. Linear molecules can line up together and the van der Waals forces therefore exist over the whole length. Branched or spherical molecules are in contact over a smaller area. Therefore, the van der Waals forces are smaller and the boiling points are lower. For example, consider these isomers of C_5H_{12}:

H_3C—CH_2—CH_2—CH_2—CH_3
Pentane (boiling point 309 K)

H_3C—$\underset{\underset{CH_3}{|}}{\overset{\overset{CH_3}{|}}{C}}$—$CH_3$
2,2-dimethylpropane (boiling point 283 K)

The molecules have the same mass and the same number of electrons, but pentane is a linear molecule and has a higher boiling point.

Van der Waals radii

In a solid molecular substance (e.g. iodine, sulphur) the distance between atoms in a molecule is not the same as the distance between atoms in adjacent molecules.

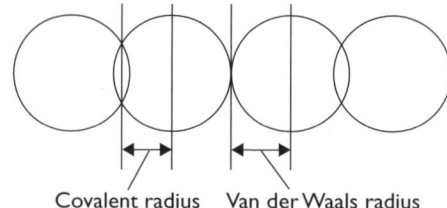

Covalent radius   Van der Waals radius

- **Covalent radius** — half the distance between the nuclei of two atoms in a molecule
- **Van der Waals radius** — half the distance between the nuclei of two atoms in adjacent molecules

Substance	Covalent radius/nm	Van der Waals radius/nm
Fluorine	0.071	0.155
Chlorine	0.099	0.180
Bromine	0.114	0.190
Iodine	0.133	0.195

Permanent dipole–dipole attractions

All molecules exert van der Waals forces due to the fluctuating electronic dipoles, but some molecules also have dipoles that are permanent. Such polar molecules always contain electronegative atoms, such as oxygen, nitrogen or chlorine. Propanone is an example of a molecule with a permanent dipole. The δ+ of one molecule will attract the δ− of an adjacent molecule. The intermolecular force of attraction will require energy to break it.

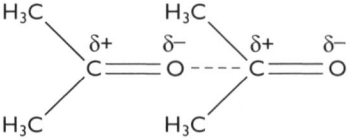

The polarity of molecules is demonstrated using the apparatus below:

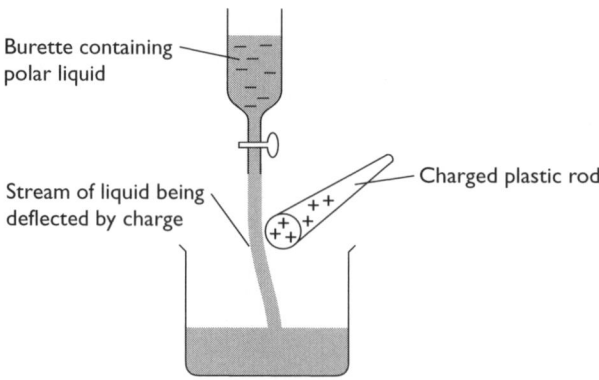

The effect of permanent dipole forces can be seen by comparing the boiling points of two substances, one polar and one non-polar, which have similar numbers of electrons:

Substance	Number of electrons	Type(s) of intermolecular force	Boiling point/K
Propanone	32	Van der Waals Permanent dipole	329
2-methylpropane	34	Van der Waals	261

Hydrogen bonding

Hydrogen bonds are the strongest type of intermolecular force. They exist only in special circumstances:
- One molecule must have a hydrogen atom which is strongly δ+, that is, attached to nitrogen, oxygen or fluorine.
- The adjacent molecule must have one of the three smallest electronegative atoms, that is, nitrogen, oxygen or fluorine.

Because of the strong δ+, the hydrogen atom is an almost naked proton. This strongly attracts the available lone pair on the electronegative atom in the adjacent molecule.

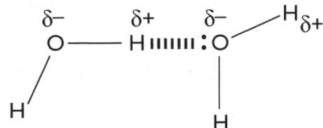

The hydrogen bond is shown as a dashed line joining the H atom in one molecule with the electronegative atom in the *adjacent* molecule. For maximum effect, the bond angle is 180°.

Significance of hydrogen bonding

Water has tiny molecules with a molar mass of $18\,g\,mol^{-1}$ and a total of 10 electrons. Methane is a comparable molecule in terms of size and number of electrons. Yet water has a boiling point of 373 K; methane has a boiling point of only 109 K!

A graph of boiling point against period number can be drawn for the group 6 hydrides.

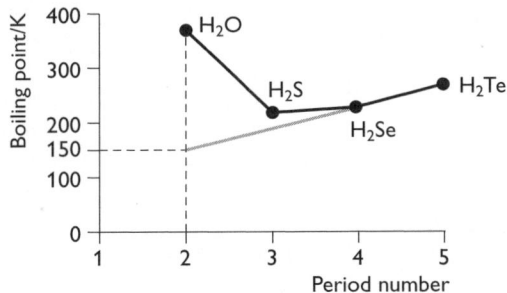

Following the trend of the straight line from period 5 down through period 4, the boiling point of water should be about 150 K. The presence of hydrogen bonds, attracting the water molecules to each other, means that considerable energy is needed to pull the water molecules *away* from each other. This is why water has a very high boiling point for such a small molecule.

Tip Be careful with your choice of words. Boiling a substance does not pull the molecules into pieces — you do not get hydrogen and oxygen when you boil water! The molecules are separated from each other because the intermolecular forces are broken.

The boiling points increase from H_2S, through H_2Se to H_2Te because the molecules have increasing numbers of electrons and therefore have greater van der Waals forces of attraction.

Examples of hydrogen bonding

- In ice, hydrogen bonding holds the water molecules in an open lattice. When ice begins to melt, the lattice collapses and the water molecules become closer to each other. This is why ice has a lower density than liquid water (icebergs float).
- Hydrogen bonding is important in explaining why some organic compounds are soluble in water. If a compound (such as ethanol) can form hydrogen bonds with water, it will dissolve.
- Hydrogen bonding is largely responsible for maintaining the three-dimensional structure of complex biological molecules such as DNA and enzymes.

Relative strengths of intermolecular forces

The relative strengths of intermolecular forces are shown in the following table.

Type of attractive force/bond	Approximate strength/kJ mol^{-1}
Van der Waals forces	3
Permanent dipole attractions	10
Hydrogen bonding	30
Typical covalent bond	400

Questions & Answers

AS Chemistry

In this section of the guide, there are seven questions which between them test all the requirements of the Unit 2 specification. They represent the kinds of questions you will get in the unit test. In contrast to the real thing, there are no lines or spaces left for the answers. Instead, the presence of a space or number of lines is indicated. The number of marks is, of course, also shown. However, taken together, these questions are much longer than a single paper, so do not try to do them all in 90 minutes.

After each question, you will find the answers of two candidates — Candidate A and Candidate B (using different candidates for each question). In each case, Candidate A is performing at the C/D level, while Candidate B is an A-grade candidate.

Examiner's comments

All candidate responses are followed by examiner's comments. These are preceded by the icon *e* and indicate where credit is due. In the weaker answers, they also point out areas for improvement, specific problems and common errors.

How to use this section

- Do the question, giving yourself a time limit of $1\frac{1}{2}$ minutes per mark; do not look at the candidates' answers or examiner's comments before you attempt the question yourself.
- Compare your answers with the candidates' answers and decide what the correct answer is; still do not look at the examiner's comments while doing this.
- Finally, look at the examiner's comments.

Completing this section will teach you a lot of chemistry and vastly improve your exam technique.

Section A

Bromine

(1) The element bromine is made by reacting chlorine with bromide ions. Bromine has several important uses.

(a) (i) Write a balanced *ionic* equation for the reaction of chlorine molecules with bromide ions. (*space*) (1 mark)

(ii) Give *one* observation you would expect to make if you carried out this reaction. (*2 lines*) (1 mark)

(b) Silver bromide can be made by reacting aqueous solutions of bromide ions and silver ions.

(i) Write an ionic equation, with state symbols, for this reaction. (*space*) (2 marks)

(ii) What would you *observe* when silver bromide is exposed to light? (*2 lines*) (1 mark)

(iii) Give a use of silver bromide that depends on this observation. (*1 line*) (1 mark)

(c) Bromine reacts with alkanes to form useful products.

(i) Complete equations 2 and 3 below to show how bromine reacts with hexane. (3 marks)

$Br_2 \longrightarrow 2Br\bullet$ equation 1
$Br\bullet + C_6H_{14} \longrightarrow C_6H_{13}\bullet + \ldots\ldots\ldots$ equation 2
$\ldots\ldots\ldots + Br_2 \longrightarrow \ldots\ldots\ldots + Br\bullet$ equation 3

(ii) Give a necessary condition for the reaction in equation 1 to occur. (*1 line*) (1 mark)

(iii) Give the formula of a free radical from the equations above. (*1 line*) (1 mark)

(iv) Name the type of bond breaking that occurs in equation 1. (*1 line*) (1 mark)

(v) Equation 1 is called an initiation reaction. What term is used to describe equation 2? (*1 line*) (1 mark)

Total: 13 marks

Candidates' answers to Question 1

Candidate A

(a) (i) $Cl + Br^- \longrightarrow Br + Cl^-$

Candidate B

(a) (i) $Cl_2 + 2Br^- \longrightarrow Br_2 + 2Cl^-$

 Candidate B scores the mark. Candidate A has not taken the hint in the question that chlorine *molecules* are required in the equation, so does not score the mark.

Candidate A

(a) (ii) The solution goes yellow.

Candidate B

(a) (ii) The solution goes from very pale green to brown.

Section A

e Both candidates score the mark. Note that it is important to specify that it is the *solution* that changes colour (rather than, for example, a precipitate being formed). A solution of bromine looks yellow or brown (or orange) depending on its concentration. Candidate B has taken the precaution of giving the starting colour as well, but this was not required.

Candidate A

(b) (i) $Ag^+(l) + Br^-(l) \longrightarrow AgBr(s)$

Candidate B

(b) (i) $Ag^+(aq) + Br^-(aq) \longrightarrow AgBr(s)$

e Both candidates score 1 mark for the correct equation. Candidate B also scores the mark for the correct state symbols. Candidate A has put (l) (liquid), rather than (aq) (aqueous solution), after both reactants, so does not score the second mark.

Candidate A

(b) (ii) It will change colour.

Candidate B

(b) (ii) It will go brown.

e Neither candidate scores. Candidate A is too vague and Candidate B is wrong. The colour change is to black, as metallic silver is formed.

Candidate A

(b) (iii) Photography

Candidate B

(b) (iii) Film

e Both candidates score the mark but they are sailing close to the wind, particularly Candidate B. 'A component of photographic film' is the best answer.

Candidate A

(c) (i) $Br\bullet + C_6H_{14} \longrightarrow C_6H_{13}\bullet + HBr$ equation 2
$H + Br_2 \longrightarrow HBr + Br\bullet$ equation 3

Candidate B

(c) (i) $Br\bullet + C_6H_{14} \longrightarrow C_6H_{13}\bullet + HBr$ equation 2
$C_6H_{13}\bullet + Br_2 \longrightarrow C_6H_{13}Br + Br\bullet$ equation 3

e Candidate A scores 1 mark for HBr in equation 2. After this he goes off the rails. There are no hydrogen atoms formed in any of the previous reactions. However, he scores a 'transferred error' mark by giving HBr as the correct compound to balance the equation with H as the reactant. Candidate B gives the correct substances and scores 3 marks.

Candidate A

(c) (ii) Light

Candidate B

(c) (ii) UV radiation

e Both candidates score the mark. Equation 1 represents a photochemical reaction that requires electromagnetic radiation to make it work. Both ultraviolet and visible light have enough energy to do this.

Candidate A

(c) (iii) Br•

Candidate B

(c) (iii) C_6H_{13}•

e Both candidates are correct and score the mark. There are two radicals in the equations; Candidate A has chosen one and Candidate B the other.

Candidate A

(c) (iv) Homolytic

Candidate B

(c) (iv) Heterolytic

e Candidate A scores the mark. A bond-breaking reaction in which radicals are formed (and the electrons go back to the *same* atoms from which they came) is called homolytic fission. Candidate B has picked the wrong word and does not score.

Candidate A

(c) (v) Substitution

Candidate B

(c) (v) Propagation

e Candidate B is correct and scores the mark. Equation 2 has a radical on each side and thus *propagates* the radical process. Candidate A has not responded to the clue to give the name of a stage in a radical reaction. (Besides, this reaction is not substitution.)

e **Overall, Candidate A scores 8 marks out of 13. Candidate B scores 11.**

■ ■ ■

Hydrogen iodide

(2) When hydrogen iodide is made by adding concentrated sulphuric acid to an iodide, many other products are formed. A purer sample of hydrogen iodide can be prepared by adding another acid to an iodide.
 (a) (i) Name the acid that is used. (*1 line*) (1 mark)
  (ii) Draw a diagram of the apparatus you would use for the preparation and collection of hydrogen iodide. (*space*) (2 marks)

Section A

(b) When sodium iodide reacts with concentrated sulphuric acid, the following reactions take place:

$2NaI + H_2SO_4 \rightarrow Na_2SO_4 + 2HI$ equation 1

$8HI + H_2SO_4 \rightarrow H_2S + 4I_2 + 4H_2O$ equation 2

(i) Describe *two* things you would *see* as these reactions occur. (*2 lines*)   (2 marks)

(ii) Write the oxidation numbers beneath the iodine and sulphur atoms in equation 2.   (2 marks)

$8HI + H_2SO_4 \rightarrow H_2S + 4I_2 + 4H_2O$ equation 2

....

(iii) Which atom has been oxidised in equation 2? (*1 line*)   (1 mark)

(iv) Equation 2 shows that 8 moles of hydrogen iodide react with 1 mole of sulphuric acid. Show how your answers to part (ii) agree with this ratio. (*3 lines*)   (2 marks)

(c) In equation 2, the states of H_2S and H_2O are shown at room temperature.

(i) H_2S is a polar molecule. Explain this statement by referring to bond polarities and the shape of the molecule. (*3 lines*)   (2 marks)

(ii) Explain why H_2Te has a higher boiling point than H_2S. (*3 lines*)   (2 marks)

(iii) H_2O has a much higher boiling point than either H_2S or H_2Te. Name the type of intermolecular force responsible. Draw a diagram to show this intermolecular force between two water molecules. (*space*)   (2 marks)

Total: 16 marks

Candidates' answers to Question 2

Candidate A
(a) (i) Hydrochloric acid

Candidate B
(a) (i) Concentrated phosphoric acid

> Candidate A is incorrect. Candidate B is correct and scores the mark. Phosphoric acid is less easily reduced than sulphuric acid so it only acts as an acid here, not as an oxidising agent.

Candidate A
(a) (ii)

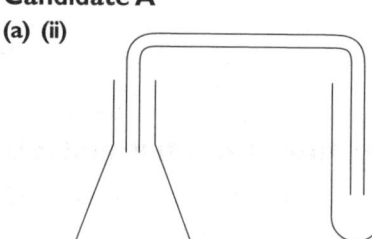

Candidate B
(a) (ii)

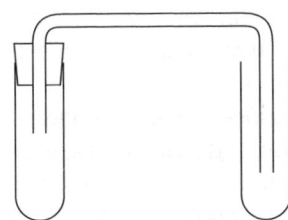

🅔 Candidate A scores 1 mark. She has drawn an acceptable apparatus but has not put a bung in the conical flask, so all the hydrogen iodide would escape! Candidate B has placed a bung in the left-hand boiling-tube and scores both marks. Both candidates have drawn the method of collection correctly.

Candidate A
(b) (i) A smelly gas and a brown colour are formed.

Candidate B
(b) (i) A purple colour in the tube (HI) and a yellow gas (H_2S)

🅔 Candidate A has not read the question thoroughly. She has correctly described two *observations* but the question asks for those *seen*. Thus the brown colour (iodine in the presence of iodide) is acceptable but the smell of hydrogen sulphide is not. She scores 1 mark. Candidate B starts well. The purple colour in the tube is another way iodine might show itself. However, he 'shoots himself in the foot' by giving extra information which, unfortunately, shows that he thinks that HI is purple (it gives steamy white fumes). This contradiction loses him the mark. Be careful not to give extra information. If the *reasons* for the observations had been required, they would have been asked for in the question. Since H_2S is colourless, Candidate B does not score.

Candidate A
(b) (ii) $8HI + H_2SO_4 \longrightarrow H_2S + 4I_2 + 4H_2O$ equation 2
          1−   6+   2−   0

Candidate B
(b) (ii) $8HI + H_2SO_4 \longrightarrow H_2S + 4I_2 + 4H_2O$ equation 2
          −1   +6   −2   0

🅔 Candidate B has all four oxidation numbers correct and scores 2 marks. Candidate A loses a mark for putting the sign after the oxidation number and so scores 1 mark only. Always put the sign *before* the oxidation number.

Candidate A
(b) (iii) Iodide

Candidate B
(b) (iii) Iodine

Section A

AS Chemistry

e Both candidates score the mark. 'Iodine' is the more accurate answer to the question but 'iodide' is acceptable.

Candidate A

(b) (iv) The iodine changes by +1 and one sulphur changes by −8.

Candidate B

(b) (iv) Iodine: eight atoms change from −1 to 0 = +8
Sulphur: one atom changes from +6 to −2 = −8

e Candidate A has not given enough detail to score 2 marks, though she does score 1 for giving the oxidation number changes of both sulphur and iodine. Candidate B has given a good answer and scores 2 marks.

Candidate A

(c) (i) The S–H bond is polar. The two bonds are not in line, so the polarities add.

Candidate B

(c) (i) The S–H bond is polar because the electronegativity of sulphur is greater than that of hydrogen. The polarities of the two bonds add to give the overall polarity of the molecule.

e Both candidates score 1 mark. Candidate A does not score the first mark because she has not explained *why* the S–H bond is polar. Her answer to the second part is brief but just scores the mark. The shape of H_2S is 'bent' like water; a full answer would have mentioned this. Candidate B scores the first mark but not the second.

Candidate A

(c) (ii) H_2Te is a bigger molecule than H_2S. Thus more energy is required to boil it.

Candidate B

(c) (ii) H_2Te has more electrons than H_2S, so its van der Waals forces are stronger.

e Candidate A's answer indicates a common fallacy and does not score any marks. However, if her first point had been 'H_2Te has a greater relative molecular mass', this *would* have scored. Remember that comparing boiling points always involves comparing intermolecular forces. Candidate B's answer is correct, for 2 marks.

Candidate A

(c) (iii) H–bonding

H——O——H⋯⋯H——O——H

Candidate B

(c) (iii) Hydrogen bonding

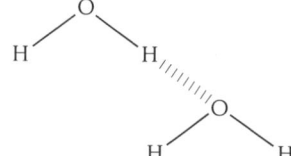

Edexcel (Nuffield) Unit 2

🖉 Both candidates score 1 mark for hydrogen bonding ('H–bonding' is not approved of, but is accepted). Candidate A makes a bad mistake by connecting adjacent hydrogen atoms, rather than a hydrogen and an oxygen. Candidate B shows a proper hydrogen bond with the correct bond angles (O–H–O, 180°; H–O–H, 107°), which are often asked for in questions of this type. He scores the second mark.

🖉 Overall, Candidate A scores 7 marks out of 16. Candidate B scores 13.

■ ■ ■

Phosgene

(3) Phosgene is a poisonous gas that is used to make various organic chemicals.

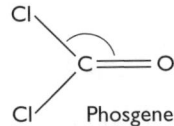
Phosgene

(a) (i) Draw a dot-and-cross diagram for a molecule of phosgene, showing the outer shell electrons only. (*space*)   (2 marks)
  (ii) Predict the numerical value of the bond angle shown in phosgene. Justify your prediction. (*3 lines*)   (2 marks)

(b) The phosgene molecule is not very polar. This is because the electronegativities of chlorine and oxygen are similar.
  (i) Explain the meaning of the term 'electronegativity'. (*2 lines*)   (1 mark)
  (ii) Mark partial charges ($\delta+$ and $\delta-$) on the molecule of phosgene below.   (1 mark)

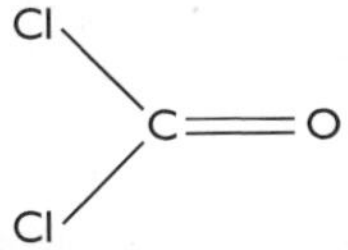

$$\text{Cl} \diagdown \atop \text{Cl} \diagup \!\! \text{C} = \text{O}$$

  (iii) Suggest why the similarity of the electronegativities of chlorine and oxygen leads to the phosgene molecule not being very polar. (*3 lines*)   (2 marks)

(c) Phosgene is manufactured by a reaction between carbon monoxide and chlorine in the presence of a catalyst. If a constant temperature is maintained, a dynamic equilibrium is established:
  $$CO(g) + Cl_2(g) \rightleftharpoons COCl_2(g)$$
  (i) The 'dot-and-cross' diagram for carbon monoxide is shown below. It shows that there is a triple bond, consisting of two covalent bonds and one dative covalent bond, joining the atoms:

$$^{x}_{x}C \!:\!\!^{x}_{x} O:$$

Explain what is meant by the term 'dative covalent bond'. (*2 lines*)   (1 mark)

Section A

AS Chemistry

(ii) **Use the data given below to calculate a value for ΔH for this reaction.** (*space*) (3 marks)

Bond	Enthalpy/kJ mol⁻¹
C≡O	+1077
C–Cl	+346
C=O	+749
Cl–Cl	+243

(d) (i) Explain the meaning of the term 'dynamic equilibrium'. (*3 lines*) (2 marks)

(ii) How would the proportion of phosgene in the equilibrium mixture shown in part (c) change if the pressure were increased? Justify your answer. (*3 lines*) (2 marks)

Total: 16 marks

■ ■ ■

Candidates' answers to Question 3

Candidate A

(a) (i) [dot-and-cross diagram of COCl₂ with Cl atoms and C=O, showing no lone pairs on Cl or O]

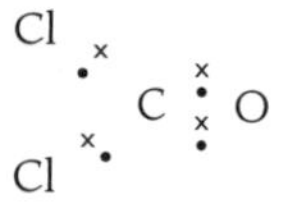

Candidate B

(a) (i) [dot-and-cross diagram of COCl₂ showing lone pairs on Cl and O atoms]

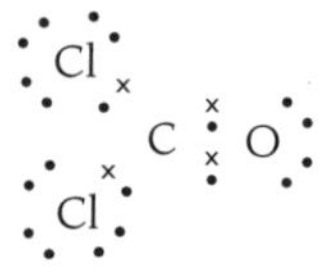

🖉 Candidate A scores only 1 mark because he has omitted the lone pairs on the oxygen and chlorine atoms. This is a common error. Candidate B has drawn a correct diagram, for 2 marks.

Candidate A

(a) (ii) 122°, since the double bond takes up slightly more room than the two single bonds.

Candidate B

(a) (ii) 120°, since there are three areas of negative charge around the carbon atom, which repel each other until they are as far apart as possible.

🖉 Candidate A scores the first mark since he has the angle about right (±2° is usually allowed). However, his reason is not correct (one of the carbon–oxygen bonds is a π-bond) and, in any case, there is not enough detail in the answer. Candidate B provides the detail needed, and scores 2 marks.

Edexcel (Nuffield) Unit 2

Candidate A

(b) (i) The power of an atom in a molecule to attract electrons to itself in a covalent bond.

Candidate B

(b) (i) The 'electron-pulling power' of an atom.

e Candidate A has given a correct definition and scores the mark. Candidate B has been rather too informal and does not score, since she has not mentioned that the atom is in a molecule.

Candidate A

(b) (ii)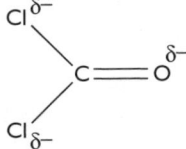

Candidate B

(b) (ii)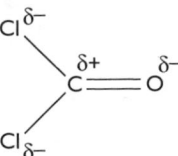

e Candidate A is nearly correct, but he has left out the δ+ on the carbon. Candidate B is correct and scores the mark.

Candidate A

(b) (iii) The molecule is symmetrical, so the charges cancel.

Candidate B

(b) (iii) The polarity of C–Cl and C–O is similar, so the bond polarities cancel.

e Candidate A scores 1 mark for the point about symmetry. Candidate B scores the first mark too, but Candidate A has put it better. However, this will only work if the polarities of the three bonds are virtually the same. Candidate B points this out, scoring the second mark.

Candidate A

(c) (i) Both electrons come from the same atom, in this case the oxygen.

Candidate B

(c) (i) A shared electron bond, where one atom gives electrons to the other.

e Candidate A gains the mark for a good answer. However, it is not essential to mention oxygen here. Candidate B has tried to indicate the origin of the term 'dative' but she has not made it clear that *both* electrons come from the same atom, so does not score the mark.

Section A

Candidate A
(c) (ii) 1077 + 243 = 1320   749 + 692 = 1441   1441 − 1320 = 121 kJ mol^{-1}

Candidate B
(c) (ii) Bonds broken: 1 × 749 = 749; 1 × 346 = 346
Total = 1095
Bonds made: 1 × 749 = 749; 2 × 346 = 692
Total = 1441
ΔH = 1095 − 1441 = −346 kJ mol^{-1}

e Candidate A has not set his work out at all well, so it is difficult to work out where he is going. He scores 1 mark for 1320 (bonds broken) and one for 1441 (bonds made). However, he then manipulates 'broken−made' the wrong way round and does not score the third mark. Candidate B has set her work out much better, so the error can easily be seen — she has used 749 rather than 1077 for the bond enthalpy in carbon monoxide. Her method is clear, so the examiner would have no hesitation in giving her 'transferred error' marks for the rest of the calculation. She scores 2 marks.

Candidate A
(d) (i) The forward and reverse reactions occur at the same time, so the concentrations of reactants and products remain equal.

Candidate B
(d) (i) The forward and back reactions occur at the same rate, so there is no change in the proportions of reactants and products.

e Candidate A is close but does not score on either point. It is not just that the forward and back reactions occur at the same time that is important, but that they occur at the same *rate*. The concentrations of reactants and products do not necessarily remain equal but they do remain *constant*. Candidate B is correct and scores both marks.

Candidate A
(d) (ii) More product would be formed.

Candidate B
(d) (ii) The reaction would be faster as there would be more collisions per second between molecules at the higher pressure.

e Candidate A scores 1 mark as he has correctly answered the first part of the question. However, he has left out the second part, the justification of the answer — that there are fewer molecules on the right-hand side and these would exert less pressure, so the equilibrium moves this way to oppose the change applied. Candidate B has provided a good answer to the question, 'How would the rate of achievement of equilibrium change with increased pressure?' Unfortunately, this was not the question asked and Candidate B fails to score. Be careful, as it is easy to confuse rate and equilibrium position in such questions.

e **Overall, Candidate A scores 8 marks out of 16. Candidate B scores 11.**

Cracking

(4) Cracking reactions are important in the petroleum industry because they make more useful hydrocarbons from less useful ones. An example of a cracking reaction is:

$$CH_3(CH_2)_{10}CH_3 \longrightarrow \underset{\underset{CH_3}{|}}{CH_3CH(CH_2)_2}\underset{\underset{CH_3}{|}}{CHCH_3} + CH_3CH={\!=}CHCH_3$$

Dodecane   Compound X   Compound Y

(a) (i) Name compounds **X** and **Y**. (*2 lines*)   (2 marks)
    (ii) Give the *molecular* formula of compound **X**. (*1 line*)   (1 mark)
(b) Draw a labelled diagram of the laboratory apparatus and materials you would use to crack a liquid alkane and to collect the gaseous product. (*space*)   (4 marks)
(c) Suggest why compound **X** is more useful as a component of petrol than dodecane. (*2 lines*)   (1 mark)
(d) (i) Compound **Y** exists as two geometric isomers. Draw the *displayed formula* of the *cis*-form. (*space*)   (1 mark)
    (ii) The C–H single bonds in the structure can be described as σ-bonds with the electrons between the atoms. Describe the C=C double bond in a similar way. (*3 lines*)   (2 marks)
    (iii) Explain why *cis–trans* isomerism only occurs when there is a C=C double bond in the molecule. (*3 lines*)   (1 mark)
(e) Compound **Y** reacts with bromine.
    (i) Describe what you would *see* when this reaction occurs. (*2 lines*)   (1 mark)
    (ii) Give *two* words that describe the mechanism of this reaction. (*1 line*)   (1 mark)
    (iii) Complete the diagram below to show how this reaction occurs. Show partial and complete charges on the relevant atoms and give the formula of the product.   (3 marks)

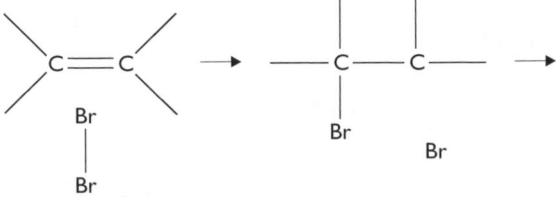

Total: 17 marks

Candidates' answers to Question 4

Candidate A
(a) (i) Compound X = 2,5-dimethylhexane; compound Y = butene

Candidate B
(a) (i) Compound X = 2,5-methylhexane; compound Y = but-2-ene

Section A

e Candidate A scores 1 mark for 2,5-dimethylhexane. Butene exists as but-1-ene and but-2-ene, compound Y being the latter. Candidate A has not specified which isomer of butene is present, so she does not score this mark. Candidate B has done this but has failed to describe the alkane as *di*methyl, so he also scores 1 mark.

Candidate A
(a) (ii) C_4H_9

Candidate B
(a) (ii) C_8H_{18}

e Candidate A has given the *empirical* formula, so does not score. Candidate B is correct, for 1 mark.

Candidate A
(b)

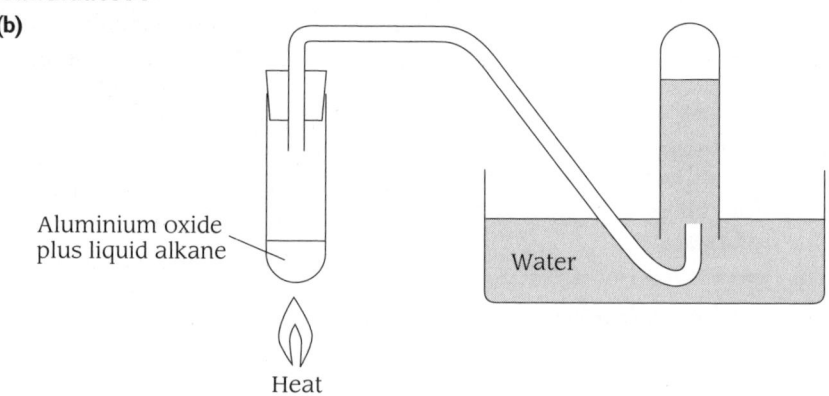

Candidate B
(b)

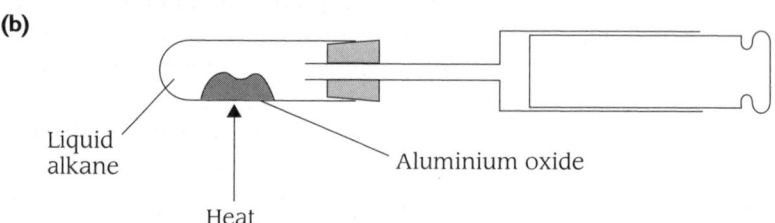

e Candidate A scores 1 mark for collecting the gas over water. However, she has confused the porous support required for the alkane with the catalyst aluminium oxide. Heating it all together is unlikely to crack the alkane, so she does not score any further marks. Candidate B scores the collection mark for a gas syringe. He also scores marks for the catalyst and heating it. However, he does not make it clear how the liquid alkane is kept at the end of the tube (a suitable absorbent should have been used), so he scores 3 out of 4 marks.

Candidate A
(c) It is more volatile.

Candidate B
(c) It is more branched, so less likely to knock.

✎ There are several possible answers here and each candidate has given an acceptable one. They both score the mark.

Candidate A
(d) (i)

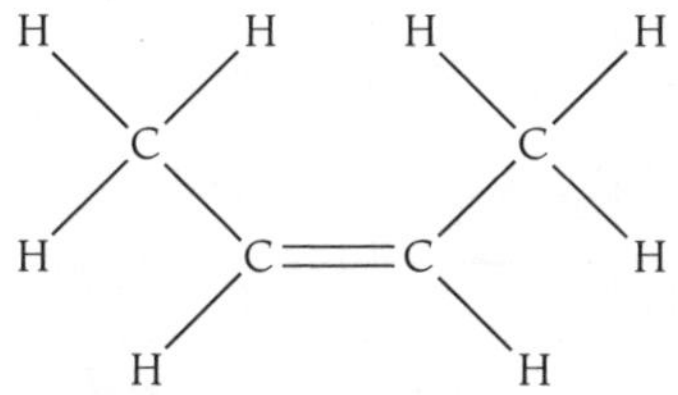

$$\begin{array}{c} H\quad\quad H\quad\quad\quad H\quad\quad H \\ \diagdown\;\diagup\quad\quad\quad\quad\diagdown\;\diagup \\ C\quad\quad\quad\quad\quad\quad C \\ \diagup\quad\diagdown\quad\quad\diagup\quad\diagdown \\ H\quad\quad C=C\quad\quad H \\ \diagup\quad\quad\quad\diagdown \\ H\quad\quad\quad\quad\quad H \end{array}$$

Candidate B
(d) (i)

$$\begin{array}{c} H_3C\quad\quad\quad\quad CH_3 \\ \diagdown\quad\quad\quad\diagup \\ C=C \\ \diagup\quad\quad\quad\diagdown \\ H\quad\quad\quad\quad H \end{array}$$

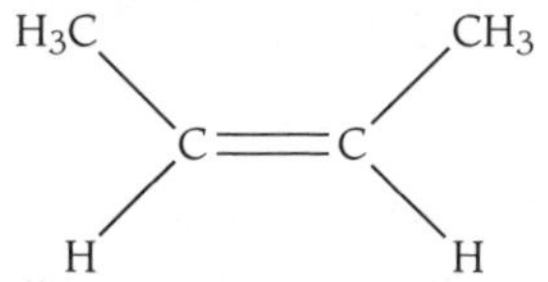

✎ Candidate A has given the correct structure and scores the mark. Candidate B has also shown the *cis-* structure but he has not noticed that a displayed formula is required, so he does not gain the mark.

Candidate A
(d) (ii) One sigma- and one pi-bond

Candidate B
(d) (ii) One sigma-bond and one pi-bond, with the electrons above and below the line of atoms.

✎ Candidate A scores 1 mark but she has not described the π-bond for the second mark. Candidate B has done this and scores 2 marks.

Candidate A
(d) (iii) There is a lack of free rotation around the C=C bond.

Candidate B
(d) (iii) The pi-bond stops the carbon–carbon bond rotating.

✎ Both candidates score the mark.

Candidate A
(e) (i) The bromine goes clear.

Section A

Candidate B

(e) (i) The bromine goes from brown to colourless.

e Candidate A has made a common error. 'Clear' is not the same as 'colourless', so she does not score. Candidate B has given a careful answer (mentioning the starting colour, which is always advisable) and scores the mark.

Candidate A

(e) (ii) It is a fast addition reaction.

Candidate B

(e) (ii) Electrophilic addition

e Candidate A notices that it is an addition reaction, but 'fast' is not a suitable word to describe a mechanism. She does not score the mark. Candidate B is correct, for 1 mark.

Candidate A
(e) (iii)

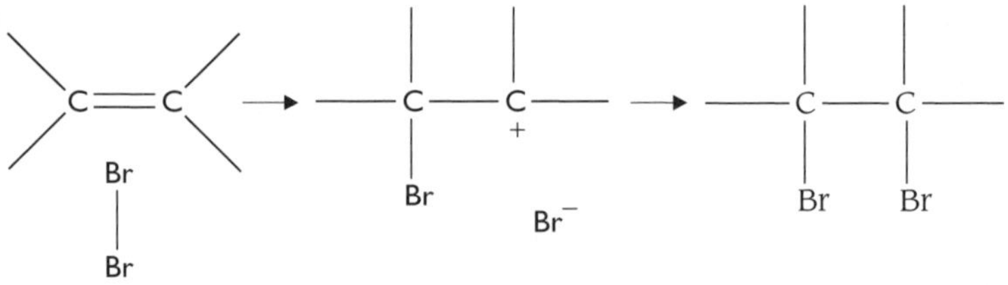

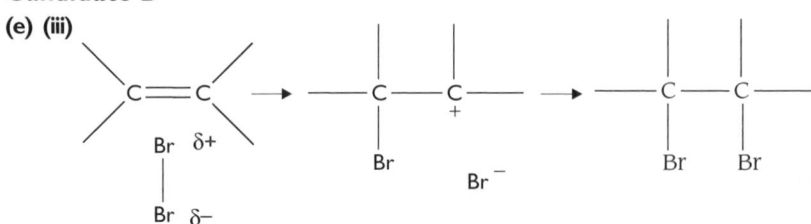

Candidate B
(e) (iii)

e Candidate A gains 1 mark for the product and 1 mark for the correct charges on the middle structure. She fails to show the partial charges on the bromine molecule (caused by the repulsion of the electrons by the π-bond), so she does not gain the third mark. Candidate B is completely correct and scores 3 marks.

e **Overall, Candidate A scores 8 marks out of 17. Candidate B scores 14.**

Halogenoalkanes

(5) Some reactions of a halogenoalkane are shown in the diagram below:

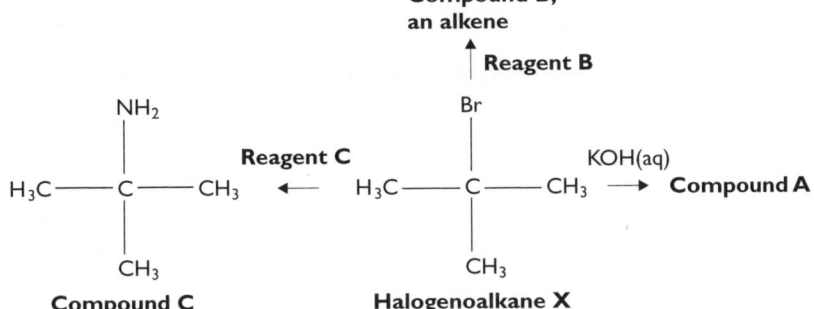

(a) Name halogenoalkane X. (*1 line*) (1 mark)
(b) (i) Draw a *displayed formula* for compound A and give its name. (*space, 1 line*) (2 marks)
(ii) The reaction to form compound A is called nucleophilic substitution. Explain what is meant by the term 'nucleophile'. (*3 lines*) (2 marks)
(c) (i) What substance(s) would make up reagent B? (*2 lines*) (2 marks)
(ii) Give the structural formula and the name of compound B. (*space, 1 line*) (2 marks)
(iii) Name the type of reaction by which compound B is formed. (*1 line*) (1 mark)
(d) (i) What substance(s) would be used to make reagent C? (*2 lines*) (2 marks)
(ii) State the conditions needed for the reaction to occur. (*2 lines*) (1 mark)
(iii) Name the *functional group* in compound C. (*1 line*) (1 mark)
(e) (i) A student treats a few drops of halogenoalkane X with a few drops of silver nitrate. Name the precipitate that is formed and state its colour. (*2 lines*) (2 marks)
(ii) The student repeats the experiment with the halogenoalkane shown below:

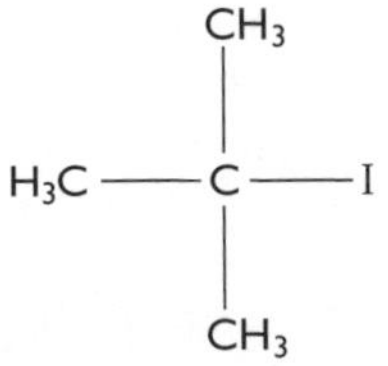

$$H_3C - \underset{\underset{CH_3}{|}}{\overset{\overset{CH_3}{|}}{C}} - I$$

The formation of the precipitate is faster. The student states that the C–I bond is less polar than the C–Br bond and is surprised by the result. What is the explanation for the difference in rates? (*1 line*) (2 marks)
(iii) The student repeats the experiment with another bromoalkane, which is an isomer of halogenoalkane X. The reaction goes much more slowly than with X. Suggest the formula of the isomer used. (*1 line*) (1 mark)

Total: 19 marks

Section A

Candidates' answers to Question 5

Candidate A

(a) 2-bromobutane

Candidate B

(a) 2-bromo-2-methylpropane

> Candidate A has failed to realise that 2-bromobutane has four carbon atoms *in a row*. Candidate B is correct and scores the mark.

Candidate A

(b) (i)

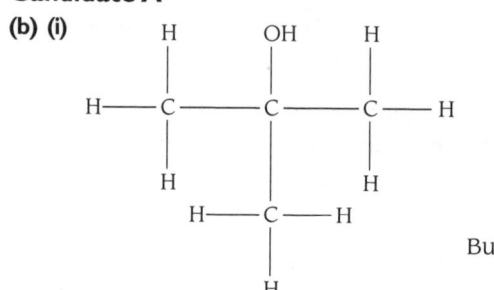

Butan-2-ol

Candidate B

(b) (i)

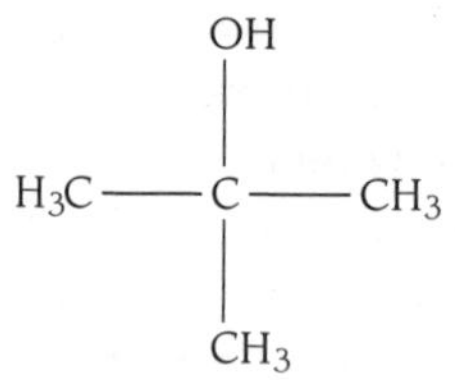

H₃C—C(OH)(CH₃)—CH₃

2-hydroxy-2-methylpropane

> Candidate A has the structure correct and scores 1 mark. Unfortunately he has made a similar error in naming the compound as he did in part (a). There is no 'transferred error' allowed here, as the names are not that similar. Candidate B does not score the first mark as she has not given the *displayed* formula. She has also forgotten that alcohols are named using 'ol' at the end, so the name should be 2-methylpropan-2-ol. Therefore, Candidate B fails to score.

Candidate A

(b) (ii) A nucleus lover that forms a covalent bond with a positively charged carbon.

Candidate B

(b) (ii) A negatively charged substance with a lone pair of electrons available to form a new covalent bond.

> Candidate A does not score for 'nucleus lover', but he scores 1 mark for mentioning covalent bond formation. Candidate B scores 2 marks, one for the lone pair availability and one for the covalent bond. Her answer is a bit risky, however, as not all nucleophiles are negatively charged (water, for example).

Edexcel (Nuffield) Unit 2

Candidate A

(c) (i) Potassium hydroxide

Candidate B

(c) (i) Ethanol and potassium hydroxide

🅔 Candidate A has only given part of the answer and scores 1 mark only. The potassium hydroxide must be dissolved in alcohol (ethanol) to give the elimination reaction to compound B, rather than compound A. Candidate B scores both marks.

Candidate A

(c) (ii) $CH_3CH(CH_3)CH_2$
Methylpropene

Candidate B

(c) (ii) 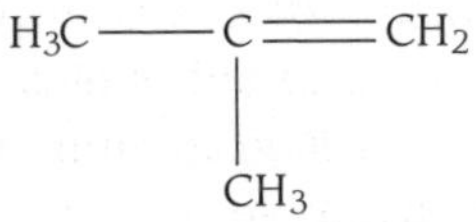
$$H_3C-C(CH_3)=CH_2$$
2-methylpropene

🅔 Candidate A has made the mistake of trying to give a condensed structural formula. He then makes another mistake by putting a hydrogen atom on the middle carbon and so loses the mark. Methylpropene is correct, for 1 mark. Candidate B has expanded the structure slightly, so she has less chance of making a mistake. Her structure is correct, so she scores the first mark. She also scores the second mark, although the '2–' is not really necessary.

Candidate A

(c) (iii) Elimination

Candidate B

(c) (iii) Loss of HBr

🅔 Candidate A is correct and scores 1 mark. Candidate B is correct in stating that HBr has been lost, but the question asks for the *type* of reaction, so she does not score the mark.

Candidate A

(d) (i) Ammonia

Candidate B

(d) (i) Ammonia and alcohol

🅔 Candidate A scores 1 mark for ammonia. Candidate B takes the hint from the way the question is phrased and the fact that there are 2 marks available and gives another answer. 'Alcohol' is just acceptable; 'ethanol' would be better. She scores 2 marks.

Candidate A

(d) (ii) Reflux

Section A

Candidate B

(d) (ii) Heat under pressure

e Candidate A has fallen back on a method that often works, but unfortunately not here! For the reaction to take place, the heating has to be under pressure. Candidate B scores the mark; Candidate A does not.

Candidate A

(d) (iii) Ammine group

Candidate B

(d) (iii) Amine group

e Candidate B is correct, for 1 mark. Candidate A has spelt the name of the group incorrectly. Spelling mistakes are often not penalised, unless they are technical terms, as here. Therefore, he does not score the mark.

Candidate A

(e) (i) Silver bromide; cream

Candidate B

(e) (i) Silver bromide; yellow

e Candidate A gains 2 marks for a completely correct answer. Candidate B scores 1 mark only. Yellow is too deep a colour to describe silver bromide, which is sometimes described as off-white.

Candidate A

(e) (ii) The bond energies differ.

Candidate B

(e) (ii) The bond energy of C–I is less than that of C–Br.

e Candidate A is correct but does not give a full enough explanation, so he gains only 1 mark. Candidate B is completely correct, for 2 marks.

Candidate A

(e) (iii) $CH_3CH_2CH_2CH_2I$

Candidate B

(e) (iii) CH_3–CH_2–CH_2–CH_2Br

e Candidate A has the right idea — the answer is a straight-chain halogenoalkane, as these react more slowly than branched halogenoalkanes. Unfortunately, he has not read the question carefully and has given an isomer of the compound in part **(e)(ii)** rather than compound X. Therefore, he does not score the mark. Candidate B is correct, for 1 mark.

e **Overall, Candidate A scores 9 marks out of 19. Candidate B scores 15.**

Nitrogen and ammonia

(6) Nitrogen is an unreactive gas. However, there are some reactions in which nitrogen is turned into its compounds. One of these is the formation of ammonia:
$$N_2(g) + 3H_2(g) \rightleftharpoons 2NH_3(g) \quad \Delta H = -92 \text{ kJ mol}^{-1}$$

(a) What feature of the bonding in nitrogen molecules makes it unreactive? (*2 lines*) (1 mark)

(b) The rate at which equilibrium is achieved increases with temperature. Explain this. (*3 lines*) (2 marks)

(c) How does the proportion of ammonia in the equilibrium mixture change if the temperature is raised? Justify your answer. (*4 lines*) (3 marks)

(d) This reaction is catalysed by finely divided iron. How, if at all, would the proportion of ammonia in the equilibrium mixture change when the catalyst is used? Justify your answer. (*2 lines*) (1 mark)

(e) Part of an energy profile for this reaction is shown below:

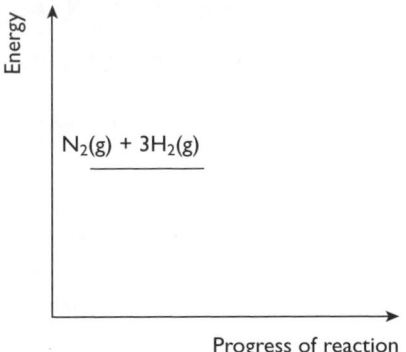

Complete the profile to show:
- the products
- the progress of the catalysed *and* uncatalysed reactions
- labelled arrows to show the activation energy of the catalysed *and* uncatalysed reactions (4 marks)

Total: 11 marks

■ ■ ■

Candidates' answers to Question 6

Candidate A
(a) The triple bond

Candidate B
(a) The strong bond between the nitrogen atoms

Section A

> Both answers are acceptable, so each scores the mark. If strong bonds have to be broken, this often means the activation energy is high, so reactions are slow.

Candidate A

(b) There are more collisions as the temperature is raised.

Candidate B

(b) As the temperature increases, there are more collisions with energy greater than the activation energy.

> Candidate A scores 1 mark. However, it is important to relate the increase in rate to the proportion of molecules with energy greater than the activation energy. Candidate B does this and scores both marks.

Candidate A

(c) Since the reaction is exothermic, less ammonia is produced.

Candidate B

(c) The proportion of ammonia is smaller since the forward reaction is exothermic and the equilibrium position moves to oppose the change.

> There are 3 marks available here, so a detailed answer is required. Candidate A scores 2 marks for saying that there is less ammonia and relating this to the exothermic reaction. Candidate B also scores the third mark for the logical link in terms of the equilibrium position moving to oppose the change.

Candidate A

(d) There would be no change in the proportion of ammonia formed. The equilibrium would be set up faster.

Candidate B

(d) There would be no change since the catalyst speeds up both the forward and the back reactions to the same extent.

> Only Candidate B scores the mark. He justifies his prediction correctly. Candidate A has written good chemistry but, unfortunately, she has not answered the question.

Candidate A

(e)

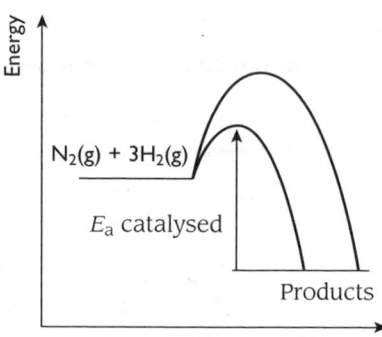

Candidate B
(e)

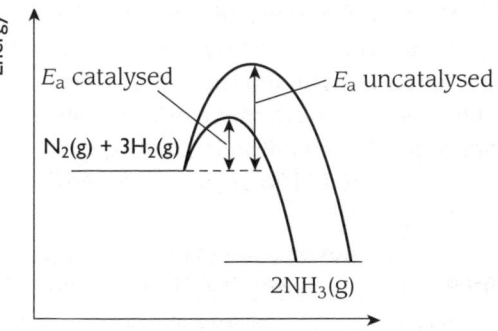

🅔 Candidate A scores 3 marks for the products being at a lower energy level than the reactants, the correct shape of the progress curve and the lower curve for the catalysed reaction (just labelled enough by the inaccurate E_a arrow). Candidate B also scores 3 marks for these points. The arrows are in the right place, but they are double-headed, rather than being upward-pointing to indicate that E_a is always endothermic.

🅔 **Overall, Candidate A scores 7 marks out of 11. Candidate B scores 10.**

Comprehension

(7) Read the passage below straight through once, and then once again more carefully, before answering the questions.

The flexibility of polymers

The second half of the twentieth century was notable for the production of 'man-made' polymers, which now make up so many things that we use in our everyday lives, from fabrics through domestic utensils to computer components. Although these polymers all consist of chains of carbon atoms, sometimes interspersed with other atoms, they have a variety of physical properties, making them suitable for different purposes. One property that greatly affects their use is flexibility.

Chemically, polymers fall into two types, addition polymers and condensation polymers. Addition polymers are usually made from monomers that are derivatives of ethene. For example, polychloroethene (PVC) is made by polymerising the monomer chloroethene:

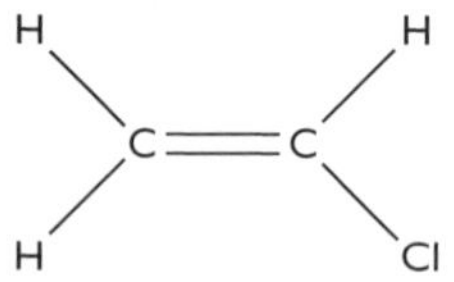

Chloroethene monomer 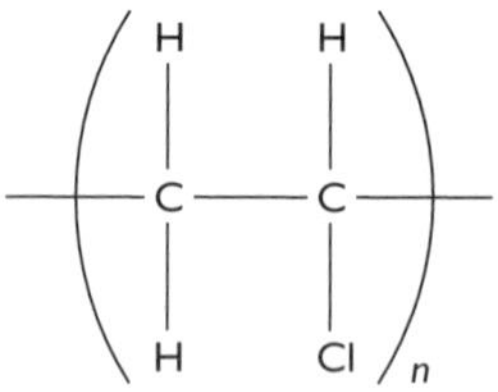   PVC polymer

Condensation polymers are made by the elimination of water molecules between monomers. This results in such polymers as nylon and poly(esters):

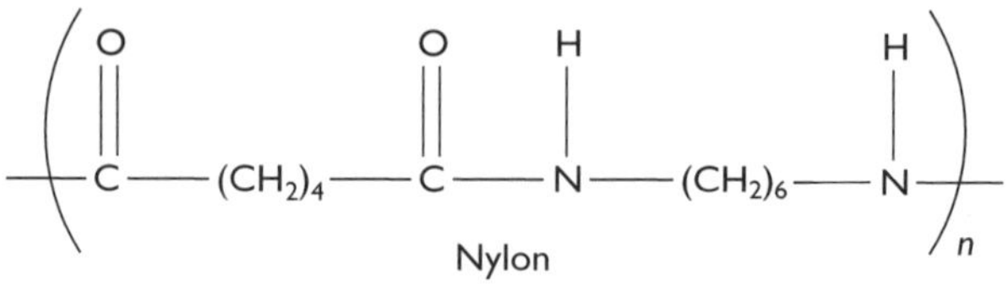

Nylon

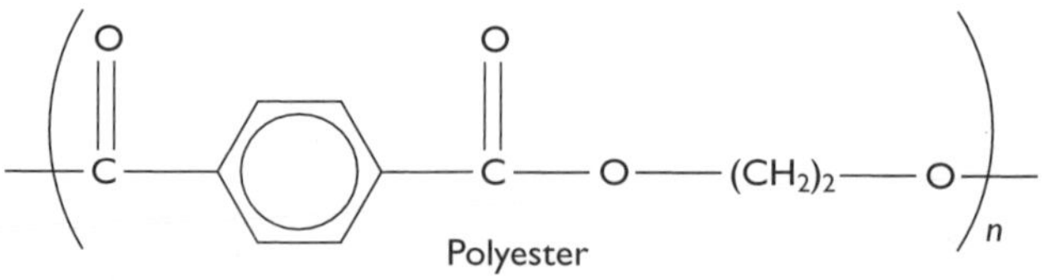

Polyester

The flexibility of a polymer depends mainly on how easily the polymer chains can slide over each other. All the polymers described above are **thermoplastic** — they soften when warmed. This is because they have only weak intermolecular forces (such as van der Waals forces) between the chains. **Thermosetting** polymers, such as those used in light sockets, are made in moulds and have covalent bonds linking the chains. Thus they are giant covalent structures (as is silica). In thermosetting polymers, the chains cannot slide at all. The structures are completely rigid and do not soften on heating.

In thermoplastic polymers, the ability of chains to slide over one another is determined by the intermolecular forces between the chains. Poly(ethene) has only van der Waals forces between the chains and is more flexible than PVC, which also has dipole–dipole forces. Polyesters also have dipole–dipole forces between the chains, which makes them more flexible than nylon, which has hydrogen bonding.

Another major factor that determines flexibility is the size of the side-groups. Thus poly(ethene) is more flexible than perspex, which has bulky side-groups sticking out from the chains.

$$\left(\begin{array}{c} H \\ | \\ -C- \\ | \\ H \end{array} \begin{array}{c} CH_3 \\ | \\ -C- \\ | \\ COCH_3 \\ \| \\ O \end{array} \right)_n$$

Perspex

These bulky side-groups prevent the chains from moving past each other so easily and therefore reduce flexibility.

PVC is available in 'plasticised' and 'unplasticised' forms. For example, unplasticised PVC is used in drainpipes and double-glazing units. It is just the polymer. PVC containing an added 'plasticiser' is used for applications where more flexibility is needed, for example food-wrap. Some plasticiser molecules simply push the chains apart, enabling them to slide over each other more easily. There are concerns that such molecules may dissolve from the food-wrap into fatty foods and may be harmful to health.

Another way of plasticising PVC is to 'copolymerise'. This involves adding a little of another monomer, for example ethenyl ethanoate, to the chloroethene before polymerisation, so that every so often in the chain a molecule of plasticiser is incorporated. This again has the effect of pushing the chains apart and reducing the strength of the intermolecular forces between them.

Ethenyl ethanoate

484 words

AS Chemistry

Section B

(a) Suggest why thermosetting polymers are used to make light fittings. (1 mark)
(b) Explain the meaning of the term 'giant covalent structure'. (1 mark)
(c) Draw the structure of the *monomer* of perspex. (1 mark)
(d) Name the strongest type of intermolecular force that would exist between perspex chains. (1 mark)
(e) Draw a diagram of parts of two nylon chains, joined together by hydrogen bonds. (1 mark)
(f) Draw part of a plasticised **PVC** *chain* made from one chloroethene molecule and one ethenyl ethanoate molecule. (2 marks)
(g) Describe, *in no more than 120 words*, the factors that affect the flexibility of polymers. (8 marks)
 - Do not summarise the whole passage or include equations in your summary.
 - You will be given credit for an answer written in good English, using complete sentences.
 - You must take care to use technical words correctly and to use chemical names rather than formulae.
 - Avoid copying long sections from the original passage.
 - Numbers, standard abbreviations, units and hyphenated words all count as one word. A title does not form part of your word total.
 - State the number of words you have used at the end of your summary. You will be penalised if you use more than 120 words.

Total: 15 marks

■ ■ ■

Candidates' answers to Question 7

Candidate A
(a) Because they are not flexible.

Candidate B
(a) Because they will not soften when they get hot.

 Candidate A has taken up the theme of the question but he is going in the wrong direction. The important clue is two lines before the reference to light sockets '*thermoplastic...soften when warmed*'. Candidate B has spotted this and given the correct answer, so she scores the mark.

Candidate A
(b) The covalent chains are bonded to each other by more covalent bonds.

Candidate B
(b) All the atoms in the structure are joined to others by covalent (electron-sharing) bonds.

Edexcel (Nuffield) Unit 2

e Both candidates have given acceptable answers here. Candidate B has been sensible to mention 'atoms', though she need not have explained what covalent bonds are.

Candidate A

(c)
```
   H        CH₃
   |         |
   C ——————— C
   |         |
   H         COCH₃
             ‖
             O
```

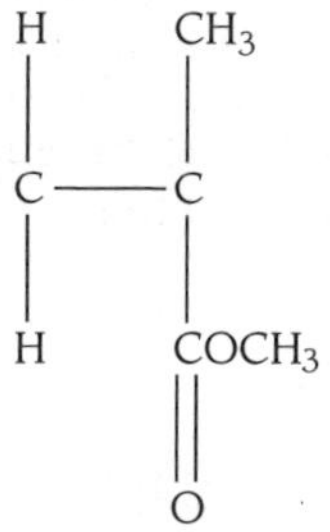

Candidate B

(c) 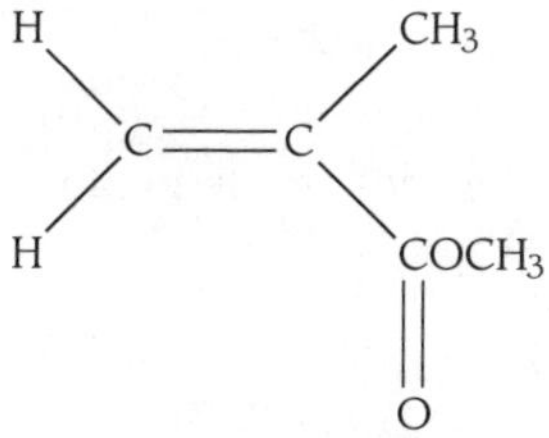
```
   H          CH₃
    \         /
     C ===== C
    /         \
   H           COCH₃
               ‖
               O
```

e Candidate A is nearly right but he has omitted the double bond, so does not score. Candidate B scores the mark.

Candidate A

(d) Dipole–dipole

Candidate B

(d) Permanent dipole–permanent dipole interactions

e Candidate A's answer is rather brief but gains the mark. Candidate B's answer is more complete, for 1 mark.

Candidate A

(e)
$$\left(\begin{array}{c} O \\ \| \\ -C-(CH_2)_4-C-N-(CH_2)_6-N- \\ \| \\ O \quad\quad H \quad\quad H \end{array} \right)_n$$

$$\left(\begin{array}{c} O \\ \| \\ -C-(CH_2)_4-C-N-(CH_2)_6-N- \\ \| \\ O \quad\quad H \quad\quad H \end{array} \right)_n$$

71

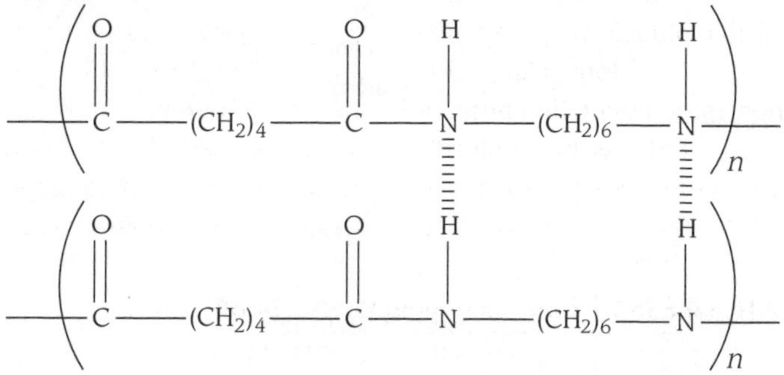

Section B

Candidate B
(e)

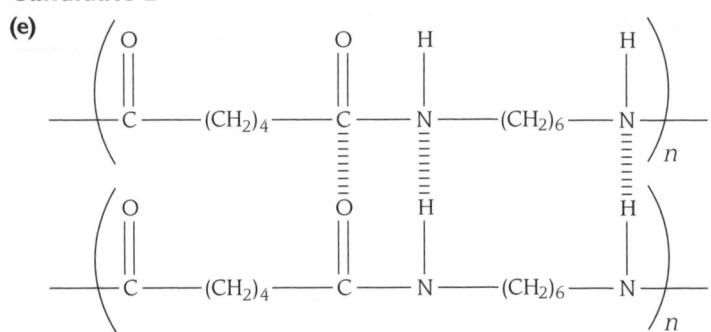

✎ Candidate A scores the mark. He has answered the question by showing more than one correctly placed hydrogen bond. Candidate B realises that the oxygen atom on the C=O can also be involved in hydrogen bonding. However, it can only bond to a hydrogen atom in O–H or N–H, so she should have turned one chain upside-down to achieve this. By showing the extra erroneous hydrogen bond she contradicts the correct detail she has already given for the other hydrogen bonds, and loses the mark.

Candidate A
(f)

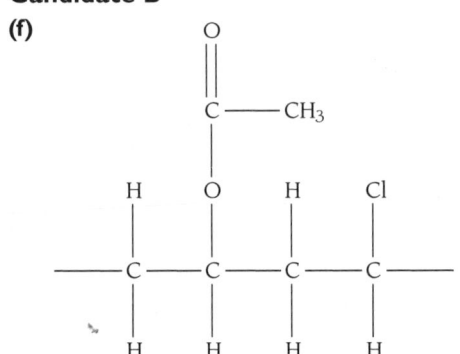

Candidate B
(f)

Edexcel (*Nuffield*) Unit 2

✏️ Candidate A has shown a dimer of chloroethene and ethenyl ethanoate, which is not what the question requested. However, he scores 1 mark. Candidate B's structure is correct, for 2 marks.

Candidate A

(g) There are two types of polymer, addition and condensation. The former (e.g. PVC) are made from unsaturated monomers, and the latter are made by eliminating water between molecules.

There are two forms of PVC, unplasticised and plasticised. Unplasticised PVC is just the polymer on its own really. Plasticised PVC is a copolymer with ethyl ethanoate. The side-chains push the chains apart. Or it can have molecules in it to push the chains apart, but these might be poisonous.

The flexibility of a polymer depends mainly on how easily the polymer chains can slide over each other. Chains which have strong intermolecular forces (for example dipole–dipole interactions) are less flexible, for example $(CH_2-C(CH_3)-COOCH_3)_n$. This also has bulky side-chains that get in the way.

123 words

Candidate B

(g) Why are polymers flexible?

This depends on the intermolecular forces between the polymer chains. Thermosetting polymers that have only covalent bonds cannot flex at all. Thermoplastic polymers' flexibility depends on the intermolecular forces between the chains. Those with hydrogen bonds, for example nylon, are least flexible; next come dipole–dipole interactions, for example PVC; then van der Waals, for example polythene, which is the most flexible. It also depends on bulky side-chains that can stop sliding, for example Perspex.

PVC can be made more flexible by adding plasticisers. These can be added molecules that push the chains apart, or other monomers can be included which have the same effect if they have larger side-groups.

109 words

✏️ These summaries are marked by looking for *key points*, for which there are 6 marks available. There are usually more than six key points and often any six out of eight or nine will score full marks. In this case, the key points are:

(1) flexibility depends on how easily chains can slide over each other
(2) no sliding in thermosets
(3) (no sliding in thermosets) since all bonds are covalent
(4) sliding depends on intermolecular forces
(5) hydrogen bonds stronger than dipole–dipole stronger than van der Waals
(6) bulky side-chains can stop *sliding/reduce flexibility*
(7) plasticiser molecules can be added
(8) can copolymerise with other *monomers/unsaturated molecules/ethenyl ethanoate*
(9) (both) push chains apart/reduce intermolecular forces

Section B

Usually, the *essence* of the point is needed, not the exact words, though words in *italics* must be included. The solidus (/) indicates alternatives.

Candidate A scores 1 mark for each of points 1, 4 (just), 7 and 9. He does not score point 6 because, although he has mentioned bulky side-chains, he does not say they stop the sliding or reduce flexibility. Candidate B scores all the points except point 8, since she has not made it clear how the other monomers are included. She therefore scores the maximum 6 marks here.

If there are excess words, a deduction is made from the key point marks. However, Candidate A would not normally be penalised as he has only just exceeded the limit and has used less than 125 words. Candidate B has been crafty in hiding excess words in her title and referring to them by 'this' in the first sentence. There is nothing wrong with this strategy.

Candidates are then assessed for 'quality of written communication'. This is awarded for good use of technical terms in the key points, clear and concise use of English, legibility of handwriting and the logic of the order in which the points are made. The mark awarded is 2, 1 or 0. Candidate A fails to score in this category. He has included irrelevant detail (the whole of the first paragraph and 'but these might be poisonous', for example). He has used inelegant English ('really' in paragraph two, and starting the last sentence of this paragraph with 'Or'). He uses a formula, rather than the name 'Perspex' and he implies that dipole–dipole forces are the strongest intermolecular force. The answer does not have a logical structure. For instance, the first sentence of the third paragraph ought to come at the beginning of the summary. Candidate B scores 1 mark. On the whole, her answer has a good style and logical structure, with correct use of technical terms. However, the last two sentences of the first paragraph let her down. The first is not well constructed and, in the second, it is hard to see what 'it' refers to.

Overall, Candidate A scores 8 marks out of 15. Candidate B scores 13.